Hazel Ratcliffe

Hazel Ratcliffe has been machine knitting for seven years. She is a tutor in machine knitting for the Inner London Education Authority and a tutor for Knitmaster. She is also a consultant editor of *Modern Knitting* and runs a seventy-strong machine knitting club. Hazel Ratcliffe is married with two children.

Machine Knitting

line drawings by Mary French   photographs by John Warren

Pan Original Pan Books London and Sydney

Contents

My grateful thanks to all the people who have helped me with the production of this book, especially Marian Nelson who provided the basic pattern system for the patterns and unlimited advice and encouragement.

First published 1978 by Pan Books Ltd,
Cavaye Place, London SW10 9PG
© Hazel Ratcliffe 1978
ISBN 0 330 25331 X
Printed in Great Britain by
Butler & Tanner Ltd, Frome, Somerset

Foreword

Many years ago I bought my first knitting machine and with hopes high I avidly read the instruction manual and set out to create masterpieces to show off to my family and amaze my friends.

Nowhere in the instruction manual did it say that the work would suddenly drop off the machine with a will of its own. Nowhere did it say that my husband would have to be eight feet tall with one arm longer than the other to fit the first sweater that I ever knitted for him.

Over the years, to everyone's relief, I have improved, traded one machine for another time and again, and gained experience. I began teaching machine knitting to others both in their homes and at evening classes. Time after time people have asked me to recommend a book to them to help them avoid the first pitfalls and bring the techniques together to see a garment through from beginning to end. Expert knitters have been well catered for in recent publications but not so the beginner. I have tried to set down the sequences here, not to rewrite your instruction book but to try to help put the basic techniques in simple language while progressing through the stages of knitting a garment.

To avoid confusion I have limited technical points to those applicable to the Knitmaster 321, 323 and 326 but this need not worry the beginner as all the basic techniques are similar for most machines.

Every machine will have a device for holding needles whether it be front levers to I or a knob or button on another machine.

Machine knitting has provided me with countless hours of profitable enjoyment and if this book can aid you through the early problems and set you on the same happy road, the writing of it will have been worthwhile.

Note: The instruction photographs in this book show techniques illustrated on sample pieces of knitting rather than on garments being made.

Chapter 1

KNITTING TERMS AND ABBREVIATIONS

For the purpose of specific instructions I have used the Knitmaster 321, 323, and 326 punchcard model (figure 1). However, by reading the following information on the function of the various machine parts knitters will be able to relate the instructions to their particular make and model of machine.

Needle positions
A Non-working position.
B Knitting position.
C Needles knit regardless of cam setting.
D Holding position.

Cam lever
T Tuck stitch.
S Slip stitch.
O Stockinet — plain knitting.
F Fair Isle.
L Punch lace.

Figure 1 A Knitmaster 326, the latest model, which is the same as the 323 in all its basic features

Front levers, or Russel levers

I Needles will not knit in D position.

II Needles in B position will knit and any needles in C or D position will be returned to B position.

Side levers

▼ Back at this position for all knitting.

▲ Forwards at this position with cam lever on S to slip the carriage across the work without knitting.

Tension dial

Numbered from 0 to 10: the larger the number the bigger the stitch. There are two stations between each number.

ABBREVIATIONS USED IN KNITTING PATTERNS

Alt	Alternate	MY	Main yarn
Beg	Beginning	N(s)	Needles
Carr	Carriage	Patt	Pattern
CO	Cast off	Pos	Position
C on H	Cast on by hand	RC	Row counter
C on WY	Cast on with waste yarn	Rem	Remaining
Dec	Decrease	Rept	Repeat
Dc	Double crochet	R(s)	Rows
Ev	Every	Rt	Right
FF	Fully fashioned. Using triple transfer tool	St(s)	Stitches
Foll	Following	Str	Straight
Inc	Increase	TD	Tension dial
HP	Holding position. D position	Tog	Together
K	Knit	WY	Waste yarn
Lt	Left	WP	Working position. B position
MT minus 1	Main tension minus one whole number		
MT plus 1	Main tension plus one whole number		
MT minus ●	Main tension minus one dot		
MT plus ●	Main tension plus one dot		

BUYING YOUR MACHINE

Buy the best that you can afford — if the money is available buy the latest, most expensive machine and you will never regret it. On the other hand, many a happy hour and many a lovely garment has emerged from the oldest of machines. So if money is short, any machine so long as it is in good repair will serve a beginner and more than earn its keep.

If you are going to purchase a new machine, a dealer specializing in several makes will be able to give you advice on the type of machine to suit both your pocket and your needs. Many of the large department stores have sections devoted to knitting machines, but bear in mind that the demonstrator who attends you is probably employed by the manufacturer of the machine you are examining and is therefore partisan. See every machine on display demonstrated fully before making your choice.

The best buys are often secondhand machines. People who encounter early failures through not applying themselves to mastering the basic skills often become disillusioned and sell almost new machines at a fraction of the original price.

A word of warning: When buying a secondhand machine, take someone with you that knows knitting machines and let them try it for you before you part with your cash.

ACCESSORIES

Once the knitting bug has bitten you, you will not be able to resist any of the accessories that adorn the knitting shops, but very few of these are essential to the beginner.

One absolute essential is the WOOL WINDER. This invaluable little item enables you to wind your wool from the shop balls into a neat ball from which you can knit successfully, pulling the wool from the centre of the ball. The wool keeps still while you knit, instead of bobbing about all over the place and interfering with the tension of the garment. The average price of a wool winder is about £5, but the only other satisfactory way to knit is from a cone, and these are not always readily available in the type of wool you may wish to use.

Another quite important accessory is a WAX PACK. This can be bought from your knitting machine supplier. Wax candles, or better still, night lights are just as good, and cheaper.

Some wools, especially double knit and Shetland are quite 'hairy' and coarse, making the pushing of the carriage across your machine more difficult than it need be. Before knitting, wind your wool into balls, running it on the wax as you wind, and you will find that the wool goes through your machine much more easily. The wax does not affect the finished garment and usually disappears when the garment is pressed, and certainly when it is first washed.

WOOL

Obviously one cannot knit without it, but beware. It is a sad but common mistake to rush out and buy 'half a ton' of cheap double knitting wool at a sale, thinking that it will do to practise on. A garment is only as good as the materials it is made from, and rarely can you knit an alluring evening gown from something you picked up on the market for 2p a skein.

Beginners should avoid thick, cheap wool like the plague. Your machine won't like it. It will be hard work to knit and the results will be disappointing.

Industrially coned yarns are often cheap and of very good quality, but they are very fine, only 1- or 2-ply. When you are used to your machine you can run two or more threads together to make up your own plys and achieve the finish of shop-bought garments but initially stick to the ply you require in single strand. So when you set forth to knit your first garment buy a good quality 3- or 4-ply wool or mixture (avoid pure nylon as this tends to be too hard). Manufacturers are at last heeding the cries of machine knitters and are now supplying 4-ply wool on cones ready waxed which are ideal.

Finally, when you buy your wool, buy enough to knit a garment. Don't buy a few odd balls to practise on — machine knitting was never learned by knitting little something. This way you will learn as you go along and have something to show for your efforts at the end; it's bound to fit somebody!

KNITTING PATTERNS

Simplicity and commonsense are the key factors when choosing your first pattern. If possible avoid hand knitting patterns. They can be used successfully but will teach you nothing about machine knitting, and at this stage you need to learn all you can in order to progress.

There are plenty of machine patterns on the market today. Several well-known wool firms produce machine knitting as do all the leading knitting machine manufacturers.

Start with a simple, basic, one colour pattern; don't be too ambitious and tackle that evening gown just yet. Several small successes will soon give you the confidence to go on to bigger and better things, but one expensive failure could see your machine under the bed gathering dust; an all too common fate for many a sad machine.

Having chosen a pattern, read through it for possible snags or alterations. Check the sizing and make any calculations for adjustments before you start knitting. For instance, if the garment is too short, work out how many extra rows you will need to knit to achieve the right length, and then make a note of it on your pattern before you begin knitting.

Read the whole pattern through. Get a picture in your mind of what the completed garment should look like.

Try to knit with the wool suggested by the pattern, and if you cannot get exactly the colour you want in the make recommended, at least use the same ply and type of wool.

As most patterns are written for several sizes, mark in pencil the directions that apply to the size you require. This will make the pattern easier to read and prevent mistakes.

With machine knitting, precise measurements are possible, and this is why some pattern writers produce a diagram giving the exact finished measurements. If you have been used to knitting by hand you will know that quite often a pattern for 97cm (38 in) for example, will knit up to a size 102cm (40 in), but with many machine patterns the actual finished size will be given.

When searching round for an idea for your first garment, try a child's garment first. It will not take so much wool or very long to knit, so you will not get bored halfway through, and it will always fit some child.

KNITTING TABLES

Your machine must be clamped to a firm surface and if this is a proper knitting table, so much the better. They vary quite a lot in price, so shop around and scan the papers for a secondhand bargain. Some people reject the knitting table thinking that because it is narrow it will only allow room for the machine and not for all the bits and pieces you wish to have to hand, but this is not so. The table has been specially designed for a knitting machine and serves its purpose well.

There is enough room for the machine and tool kit; the wool winder will fit on the end and there is space at the other end to prop up the pattern where it can easily be read. A pattern stand can be bought from a good stationers for a few pence. *Don't* clip your pattern to the yarn brake as it will certainly interfere with your work.

There is not really enough room on the table for the wool, especially if you are knitting from large cones, and this is as it should be. The wool should be on the floor directly under the yarn brake so that it flows straight up and is not pulled either one way or another as you knit. If you have a ribbing attachment, this fits on to the table and the wool must be on the floor because the yarn brake is reversed and leans much further back.

If you are going to use a kitchen table, or other substitute, this is fine so long as it is sturdy and the machine can be clamped firmly; but try to keep your layout simple. If you succumb to the temptation to make use of the extra room you have available, a clutter soon develops and frustration follows as you try to find the tools and pattern among all the odd bits of wool, coffee cups, ashtray, etc.

WHERE TO SET UP YOUR MACHINE

One place your machine should never be is in its box. This is only allowed if you are taking it on holiday, taking it to show an interested party, or trading it in for a new machine. You will never get full use out of your machine if you put it away after each session. In a spare ten minutes you can knit an awful lot, but if you have to set it all up and find the pattern etc. you probably won't bother.

If you have the space in your house, then a room of your own, with your machine, pressing board, shelves for wool etc. is ideal, but most of us are not that fortunate. There are those with small children to keep an eye on who cannot knit peacefully upstairs while they run riot downstairs, so keep your machine where you will use it most. A corner of a room, with the wool and bits and pieces to hand in a good light (preferably daylight) works just as well.

A knitting machine does not clutter up a room if it is kept tidy. It has as much right to a place in the home as a washing machine or cooker and you wouldn't pack those up in a box and put them away every time you used them. Your machine creates a lot of interest from visitors and is as much a conversation piece as a work of art.

Have a comfortable chair. Try them out for size, picking one that gives you support and a working position higher than your machine. If you can put your hands on an office chair that swivels and adjusts then this is perfect. Again secondhand bargains can often be found.

OTHER ESSENTIALS

The following are small inexpensive items that you will probably have in your home anyway: a small pair of scissors for your tool tray, a tape measure and a waste bin for wool ends. A plastic bag taped to the end of your knitting table is one idea for helping to keep things tidy.

The last essentials are a notebook and pencil. If you want to remember it — write it down. *Be methodical*. Make a note of what pattern you are knitting and what alterations you are to make, the size, colour, type and make of wool and who the recipient of this masterpiece is going to be. So, in three months time, when Aunt Alice rings up and says, 'Will you knit me another jumper, but with a round neck, sleeves 5cm shorter and a tighter welt', you will not be panic-stricken.

CARE OF YOUR MACHINE

Like any piece of machinery, your knitting machine will serve you best if you look after it. Basically all it needs is to be kept clean, dust-free and oiled.

After completing a garment, pull out all the needles to D position, check for any bent needles and replace as necessary (your instruction book will tell you how). Use the brush provided with the machine and brush away all the dust and loose fibres. With a clean dry rag wipe the old oil from the front and back rails and the needle butts. Use the brush to get rid of any fluff under the carriage and again put a clean rag over the cams and wipe off any old oil.

To oil the machine, put the oil on a clean, dry piece of cloth. Don't squirt oil directly on to your machine. Run the oily cloth along both rails and the needle butts and along the edges of the cams. Try not to over-oil. A thin film of oil is sufficient. If there is no oil with your machine, then any light oil will suit your purpose.

Never oil the machine without first wiping off the old oil; otherwise you are wasting oil and time.

Before you start to knit. Read, read, read your instruction book and familiarize yourself with the names of all the levers and knobs, knitting positions, and what they do, before you start to knit. The information that you need is in the book somewhere if you take the time to look. Most people in their initial enthusiasm skip through the book and then struggle for ages trying to work things out for themselves, causing frustration and a waste of knitting time.

Check list: Your machine is set up. You have chosen your pattern and made any necessary adjustment. All your wool is wound ready for use; there's nothing worse than having to stop halfway up a sleeve to wind more wool. Notebook and pencil to hand, scissors, waste bin, a good light and a comfortable chair and you are ready to knit.

Chapter 2

TENSION

TENSION — how to achieve the correct stitch size — is the knitter's nightmare. Many a keen knitter has given up in despair, not because she cannot manage the mechanics of knitting but because she cannot knit anything that turns out the correct size.

First of all, you must understand that different wools and different stitch patterns knit up to different tensions. You cannot say that all 4-ply wools knit at tension 7 since even the different dyes may vary. A 4-ply Acrylic in dark brown will probably knit up much tighter than the same wool in yellow.

There are no hard and fast rules. Tension is to some degree personal preference and to a greater degree practice and experience, but there are a few basic rules which, if followed, will help to prevent too many disasters.

Most important of all — you *must* knit a tension square. The few minutes and small amount of wool it takes are well worth the effort because once you have the correct tension, you can enjoy knitting your garment knowing that it is going to be the right size. It is no good trying to measure your work while it is on the machine. It is impossible because the work is distorted and takes on quite a different shape when released from the machine.

To knit a tension square

Read your pattern and try to knit with the wool suggested. If you cannot get the exact brand than at least be sure you have the same ply and type of wool: if it is 4-ply crêpe then try to knit with 4-ply crêpe and not 4-ply Shetland.

Most patterns give a tension guide and some give a suggested tension number. If this is the case then knit your tension square as follows: If the pattern suggests you knit the garment at tension 7 and should produce 30 stitches and 40 rows to 10 cm (4 in), then using a bit of waste yarn, cast on 30 stitches and knit a few rows. Thread up with your main wool and with your tension dial at 6 knit 40 rows, then with your tension dial at 10, knit one row to mark the end of that square. With the tension dial at 7 knit 40 rows and then one row at tension 10. Set your tension dial to 7 and knit 40 rows. Change to waste yarn and knit a few rows before removing from the machine. Leave it to rest for at least an hour before measuring it. This allows the work to settle and assume its finished shape.

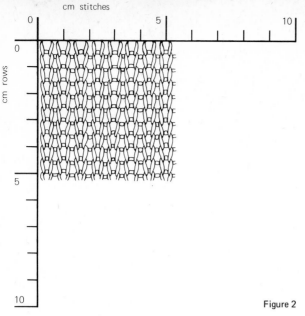

Figure 2

One of the 40 row parts of the square should measure 10cm (4 in) square (figure 2). If they are all too large or all too small, you must alter your tension dial accordingly and try again.

If, however, you can get an accurate reading for the stitch size but find that the number of rows to 10cm (4 in) is slightly out, then you can quite easily adjust the number of rows you require, e.g. if you are knitting 40 rows to 10cm (4 in) and your garment needs to be 35cm (14 in) from the bottom to under the arm, then you know you must knit 140 rows.

Generally speaking, the larger the tension square the more accurate it is.

To measure a tension square
Do measure it. Don't try to count the rows and stitches. Turn your square with the 'wrong' side uppermost, hold it as flat as you can but don't pull it or pin it, then measure it carefully. Do *not* stretch or pat the square into the required measurement. Remember that one or two stitches too many or too few in a 10cm (4 in) tension square can amount to an awful lot on a 107cm (42 in) sweater.

For a garment that is part plain and part patterned, you need to do two tension squares, otherwise you may end up with a jumper that is size 97cm (38 in) at the front and size 107cm (42 in) at the back.

Having settled for the right tension and knitted the first piece of the garment, measure it and check the size just to be sure. It takes only a few minutes to unpick a front or a sleeve, but it is a different kettle of fish to undo a whole garment when it has lovingly been pressed and sewn up.

14

Shetland wool and any wool containing spinning oil tends to shrink once it has been washed so your tension square needs to be washed before you measure it. Usually Shetland wool has to be knitted at a fairly loose tension. If your knitting pattern gives no suggested tension number, you must use the information given and hazard a guess, but after one or two attempts you soon get used to this. Reading other knitting patterns can often give you a guide to a particular type of wool.

Now all this to a beginner may seem to be a great deal of bother and trouble, not to mention a waste of wool, but this need not be if you take the right attitude to it from the outset. A correct tension square is the key to successful knitting.

Get yourself into a system. If your machine is to be a going concern and you intend to do lots of knitting, then you should have the next tension square ready before you finish the garment you are working on. The best way to stay organized is to have a preparing session — spend a couple of hours preparing your week's work. Find the patterns, wax and wind the wool and knit the tension squares. Of course make notes as you go along, e.g. JOHN'S WOOLLY — pattern book No.2, size 91cm (36 in), Supa Wash 4-ply, dark blue, tension 6, plus notes of any alterations. Put everything into a polythene bag and shelve it until you want it. This way you get the best out of your knitting time. If you find a spare half hour you can take down a bag of work and begin immediately. If, however, you have to start sorting through for a pattern, or winding the wool, or knitting the tension square it is likely that you will consider it not worth starting at all.

Tension squares need not be wasted. If you have plenty of the wool in question, then cast your tension squares on and off properly. You can collect them and use them to make a blanket of squares, or make up your own sample book to show prospective customers. If, however, you are going to need every scrap of your wool to complete the garment, bearing in mind that knitting patterns do not usually allow wool for tension squares, then as soon as you have measured the tension square, unravel it and use it to knit the welt, or for sewing up.

Keep a record of which wools knit up to which tensions; it will save you time in the future, especially if you are intending to do a lot of knitting with one sort of wool.

The tension dial on your machine speaks for itself: it controls the stitch size. The higher the number on the dial the larger the stitch produced.

The aerial tension or yarn brake controls the flow of wool to your machine and the best guide for this is to check while you are knitting. If the stitches at the end of the rows are pulling tight, then the tension is too tight. If you get loops in your work, then the tension is too loose or you have not threaded up properly.

Tension is not a great secret; it is simply a case of applying one or two general rules and taking a few extra minutes to prepare your work. After all, it takes such a short time to knit the actual garment that those few minutes of preparation are neither here nor there, but mean the difference between satisfaction with a perfect garment or disappointment.

Note: When using pattern cards, tuck stitch needs a looser stitch size than stockinet, and punch lace and slip stitch are about the same as stockinet. Fair Isle usually needs a whole stitch larger than stockinet, though this varies slightly with the pattern. A big pattern will knit up looser than a small intricate one.

When rewinding yarn that has been knitted up you must steam the yarn before you reknit it. Unravel the knitting, wind it into a hank and hold the hank in front of a steaming kettle. This will straighten out the yarn. Dry the yarn and rewind it.

To measure a tension square using the tension gauge
With the 323 and 326 Knitmaster machines there is a green rule which is used as a tension gauge.

To knit the square bring 35 needles each side of the centre to B position (70 needles in all). Make an open edge cast on and knit a few rows at different tensions until you are satisfied with the tension. Knit 20 rows. Remove the yarn and thread up with a contrast colour and knit 2 rows. Remove contrast yarn, rethread with first colour and knit 30 rows.

Move the 21st needle from either side of the centre from B to D position, put the two pieces of the contrast thread on the needles in D position and push each needle back to B position. Knit 30 rows.

Change the yarn to contrast colour again and knit 2 rows. Change yarn to main colour again. Knit 20 rows. Remove work from machine. *Make a note of the tension used.*

Allow the square to settle, about 1 hour. Put the stitch gauge with S on top between the two stitches marked with contrast thread. The number nearest the stitch on the right-hand side tells you how many stitches to 10 centimetres (figure 3).

16

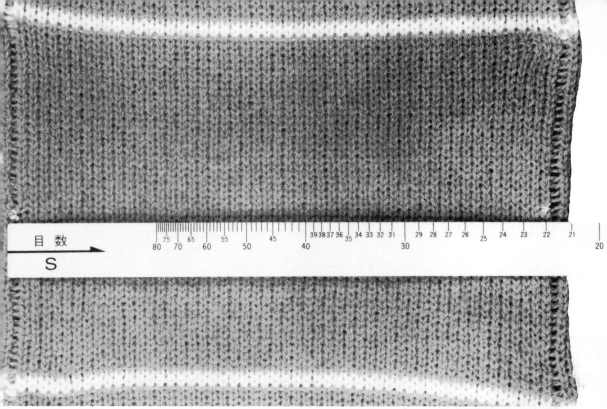

| | | 75 | | 65 | | 55 | | 45 | | 39 38 37 36 35 | 34 33 32 31 | | 29 | 28 | 27 | 26 | 25 | 24 | 23 | 22 | 21 | | 20 |
| 目 数 → | | 80 | 70 | | 60 | | 50 | | | 40 | | 30 | | | | | | | | | | | | |

S

Figure 3

Put the stitch gauge with R on top between the two sets of contrast rows. The number nearest to the row of contrast yarn tells you how many rows to 10 centimetres (figure 4).

This tension square is the most accurate method of measuring and is particularly useful when using a stitch pattern.

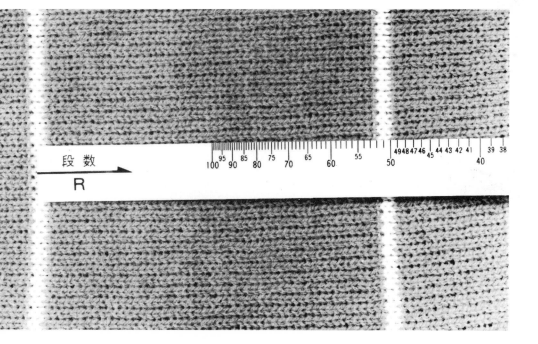

段 数 →

R

Chapter 3

CASTING ON

Before going into the various techniques of machine knitting, I must point out that with most of the operating techniques there is really no right or wrong way; mostly it is a matter of personal preference. Sometimes it is a case of whether you want speed or a professional finish, though it is usually possible to achieve both.

Open edge cast on (the waste thread method)

This method is used when it is not going to be necessary to seal the edge of your work, e.g. when you cast on with waste yarn to knit a tension square, or perhaps on a garment when you are going to remove the waste thread and pick up the stitches again for some reason.

Thread up, select your needles and knit across from right to left. Use your nylon cord and place it over the sinker pins across the complete length of your work, but on the wool between the needles and sinker pins, not on the needles themselves (figure 5). Take each end of the cord and hold it down tightly, then knit six rows. Pull out the cord and you can carry on knitting.

The nylon cord simply anchors the first row until your knitting gets going, but to repeat, this is an open, not a sealed, cast on.

Figure 5

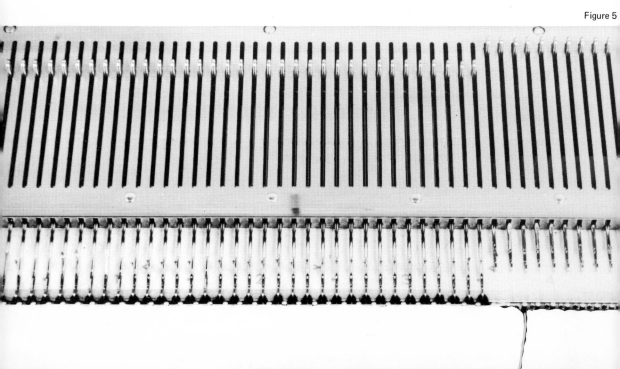

Closed edge cast on (using nylon cord)

This method is used for hems and ribs, where you are going to turn up the cast-on row to make a sealed edge.

Thread up and knit one row across with waste yarn. Hold the nylon cord across, as shown above, and then knit six rows finishing with the carriage at the left. Remove the nylon cord and break off the waste yarn. Thread your nylon cord into the carriage as if you were going to knit with it. (Only through the carriage, not through the aerial tension). Let about 15cm hang below the carriage and hold the rest loosely across the palm of your right hand, which should be above and slightly behind the carriage. With your left hand knit slowly across from left to right, letting the cord knit slowly across your work. You now thread up with your main yarn and knit your welt or hem. When this is done, using a single transfer tool, you pick up the stitches between the nylon cord stitches on the row that you knitted with the nylon cord. After picking up, remove the nylon cord. If you are doing a 1 x 1 rib, you will be hooking the stitches on to every other needle; if it is a hem, it will be every needle.

This method of threading and rethreading at first seems to be a lot of trouble, but it is the neatest way of casting on and the stitches between the nylon cord are easy to see when picking up.

Hand cast on

This is simply what it says, and has its place in machine knitting, mostly when you are not going to turn up the edge of your work on the machine, and in any case when the pattern says cast on by hand.

Pull out the required number of needles to D position, thread up your machine and make a slip knot at the end of your wool. Anchor it to the first needle on the left (carriage at the right). Wind the wool over each needle and round it in an anti-clockwise direction, that is to say, away from the carriage. Take the wool right down the needles past the latches as far as it will go (figure 6). Try not to pull it too tightly and keep the stitches even. With side levers back, front levers on II and cam lever on 0, knit one row across from right to left.

Hold the nylon cord over the work as in the waste thread method of casting on and knit a few rows. You can then

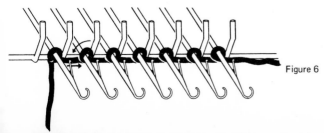

Figure 6

remove the cord and continue knitting. The purpose of this procedure is to anchor the work until there is sufficient knitting on the machine for the brushes to get purchase.

There are several other methods of casting on described in the various manuals, but these three are the basic methods and the most widely used.

WELTS

Many people, especially those who have bought a secondhand machine and who have not had any instruction, are under the terrible misapprehension that, unless you own a ribbing attachment, you cannot do a rib on your machine and they waste many knitting years doing only hems or — dare I say it — knitting the ribs by hand.

Any machine that knits will do a successful rib. It is usually called a 'Continental rib' or welt and although you cannot achieve the same results that you would on a ribber, they are, nevertheless, most satisfactory.

1 x 1 Continental rib or welt

Select the required number of needles to B position, and then by using the 1 x 1 pusher, push the second and every other needle back to A position. Thread up the machine and cast on using the waste thread method. Thread up with your main yarn and select your tension. Usually you have to go down three whole tensions to knit the welt, therefore if your main tension is 7 then your rib tension will need to be tension 4. Because you are knitting the welt and doubling it up you will have to knit twice as many rows as you actually require. Therefore for a welt 10 rows deep you will be knitting 20 rows. Knit 10 rows tension 4 and then knit one loose row at tension 10 (figure 7). This will give you a fold line at the bottom of your garment. Knit 10 rows rib tension 4 and join up the welt.

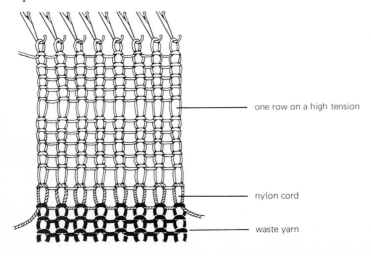

one row on a high tension

nylon cord

waste yarn

Figure 7

To join up the welt, bring all the alternate needles back to B position. Then pick up the loops of the first row knitted after the nylon cord and put them on to each empty needle. Hold the work against the sinkers with one hand and pull out the nylon cord with the other. Put your tension dial up to the main tension and knit across.

The waste thread method of casting on is best used for a welt because it makes it easy to see the pick-up row and gives a neat, closed edge when you join the welt. If you cast on by hand it is more difficult to find and pick up your stitches from the edge row and the join is not as neat.

2 x 1 welt

Select the number of stitches required and working from right to left, starting with the 3rd needle from the right, push every 3rd needle back to A position. Cast on with waste yarn and nylon cord as previously described and knit the required number of rows.

Bring every 3rd needle back to B position and pick up the loops of the first row knitted after the nylon cord as follows:
1st loop from right on to 2nd needle from right (this needle already has a stitch on it).
2nd loop on to 1st empty needle from right.
3rd loop on to 5th needle from right (this needle also has a stitch on it).
4th loop on to the next empty needle.

Continue putting the loops on to groups of 3 needles, 2 with stitches and one empty, put one loop on the second needle with a stitch and the next loop on the empty needle. Hold the work against the machine and pull out the nylon cord. Turn the tension dial to main tension and continue knitting.

3 x 1 welt

Selecting the required number of needles, starting with the 4th needle from the right, push every 4th needle back to A position. Cast on with waste yarn and nylon cord and knit the required number of rows. To pick up the loops, put the loops from the first two knitted after the nylon cord as follows:

1st loop on to 2nd needle with a stitch.
2nd loop on to 3rd needle with a stitch.
3rd loop on to 1st empty needle.

Repeat this procedure until the welt is closed. Hold the work against the machine and remove nylon cord. Turn the tension dial up to main tension and continue knitting.

Tension dial for 2 x 1 and 3 x 1 welts needs to be one full tension lower than main tension e.g. main tension 7 welt tension 6.

Note: Always use a good contrast colour for your waste yarn. This makes the pick-up row much easier to see.

HEMS

To knit a hem you can use the same principle as for a rib, except that you use every needle. Therefore when turning up the hem, you put one stitch on to every needle. It is still advisable to knit a loose row (tension 10) in the middle of your hem to give a neat edge to the finished garment. Usually you need to turn the tension dial down one dot for the hem, i.e. main tension 7, hem tension 6.

Alternative hem

A neat and easy way to knit a hem is as follows, providing your work is to appear on the machine with the wrong side facing you. The wrong side faces you when knitting plain, Fair Isle and punch lace, but when knitting tuck stitch and slip stitch and weaving your work faces you and so this method is unsuitable.

Select the required number of needles, and then with your 1 x 1 pusher, push the second and every other needle back to A position (as for a welt) (figure 8). Using your main yarn, cast on by hand and knit across from right to left. Now bring all the needles forward to D position, remembering to keep your work back against the sinkers (figure 9), then knit from left to right and continue knitting your hem. For your double up row, pick up the large loops made by the first two rows and hook then on to every other needle (figure 10).

This hem is much quicker to do than the basic method and you have no ridge where you have joined up. It is neat, flat and even the inside edge looks attractive (figure 11).

The welts and hems will look baggy whilst they are on the machine because the stitches are distorted, but don't worry about this; in Chapter 10 I will tell you how to steam them to achieve a nice finish.

I have quoted tension 10 for the fold row on welts. If the yarn is finer than 4-ply, tension 10 would be too loose. It is correct to turn the tension dial up four full tensions from the rib tension.

Note: If the hem is turned so that the purl side is the 'right' side of the garment, e.g. on a tuck stitch garment, then the centre row would need to be a tight row as opposed to a loose row in order to give a fold line.

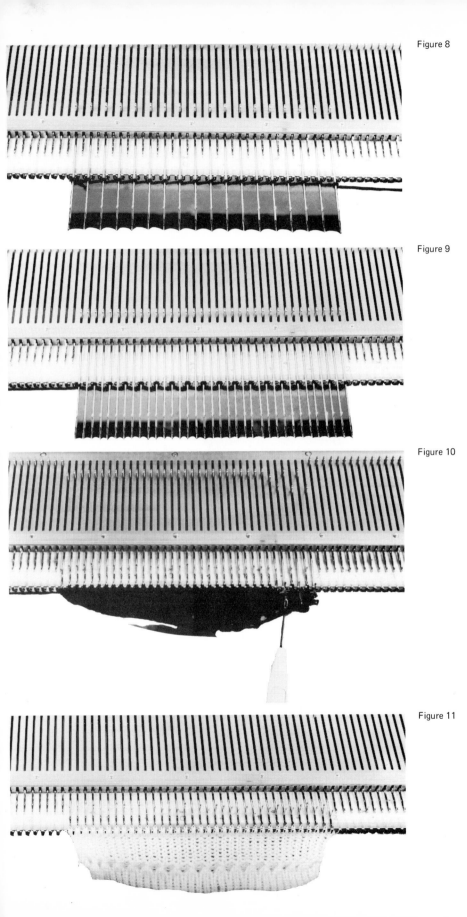

Figure 8

Figure 9

Figure 10

Figure 11

Chapter 4

KNITTING TECHNIQUES

The hem completed, you are ready to carry on and knit the body of your garment.

Set your row counter to 0 after you have completed your hem or rib; check that your tension dial is at the correct number, that the side levers are back and front levers on position II, and that the cam lever is set at 0.

Move your carriage slowly but firmly from right to left and back again, ensuring that you clear all the needles with the carriage every time. Don't try to dash along too quickly, that will come later. It is much better to knit slowly and carefully at first and get to know the feel of your machine. You need not press down on the carriage as you move it along, simply push it forwards and backwards with a regular movement.

Carriage jam when knitting stocking stitch

If for some reason your carriage should jam in the middle of a row (it may be a large kink of wool or something caught in your brushes) *never* try to force the carriage across. You will be bound to bend needles. Unscrew the brush assembly, remove it from the carriage and unthread your wool. Then, by lifting upwards on the carriage, you will be able to raise it and move it *back* to the beginning of the row without dropping any stitches. Unpick the row back to the beginning and sort out any tangles. Rethread and reassemble your carriage and you should be back in business. You can move all the needles to D position for the next row if some of the needles have the wool behind the latches. As long as the front levers are on II, the carriage will take them back to the knitting position.

To unpick a row, all you do is pull the wool away from you and then back towards you on each needle and you will find the stitch unravels. Grip the work with your left hand as you unpick with your right and in that way you will not pull the work off the machine.

If after unpicking a row, or several rows, you find that your wool is at one side of the work and your carriage at the other, then you can slip your carriage across the work without it knitting as follows: Side levers forwards, front levers on I and cam lever on S for slip stitch, you can then move your carriage across the work without it knitting. This is a very useful manoeuvre, particularly when using pattern cards, so take special note of it.

Carriage jams when using pattern cards

If the carriage jams and you are using a pattern card proceed as follows: Unscrew the brush assembly and remove it, unthread your wool. Cam lever to centre 0. Put both side levers forwards (towards you). Lift the handle to raise the carriage and slide it across the work in the direction in which you were going. Unravel the stitches already knitted and using the transfer tool put all the needles back to B position with the stitches inside the latches.

Turn the pattern card back one row and lock it. Check that the side levers are still foremost, put the cam lever to S for slip and take the carriage back across the work. Attach the brush assembly, rethread the machine, put the cam lever to the required position and put the side levers back (away from you), release the card, set the row counter back two rows and continue knitting.

Picking up a dropped stitch

If a dropped stitch runs back several rows insert the latchet tool from behind the work through a stitch several rows below the dropped stitch and pull on the latchet tool to undo the stitches down to the tool. Push the latchet tool towards you to put the stitch behind the latch. Grab the cross-thread inside the latch of the tool and pull it through the loop to reknit the stitch and then push the tool towards you again to put the new stitch behind the latch.

Continue in this way until you have reknitted to the top. Finally replace the last stitch on to the empty needle with a single transfer tool (figure 12).

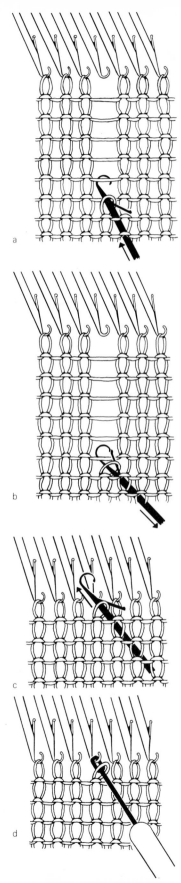

Figure 12

To transfer a stitch

This operation is probably the thing that frustrates beginners most, but it is only a matter of practice, and once mastered, you will find that you don't even think about it. At first you will find that you are all thumbs and the stitches have a will of their own; but don't be disheartened, everyone has the same problems when they start.

To transfer one stitch from one needle to another use a single eye transfer tool. Hold the tool horizontally between your thumb and index finger. Hook the tool over the needle in question and pull it out to D position (figure 13). This will put the stitch behind the needle latch. Push the needle back to A position and this transfers the stitch from the needle to the transfer tool (figure 14). Lift the tool from that needle and put the stitch on to the new needle (figure 15). To get the stitch from the tool to the needle, hook the tool over the end of the needle and pull the needle through the stitch rather than trying to wriggle the stitch on to the needle (figure 16). Whilst you are operating the tool with your right hand, hold the edge of your knitting with your left hand close to the part of the work you are operating on. Holding the work ensures that you do not drag it off the machine.

Basically, to recap the four movements:
needle out to D
needle in to A
lift transfer tool
transfer the stitch.

Figure 13

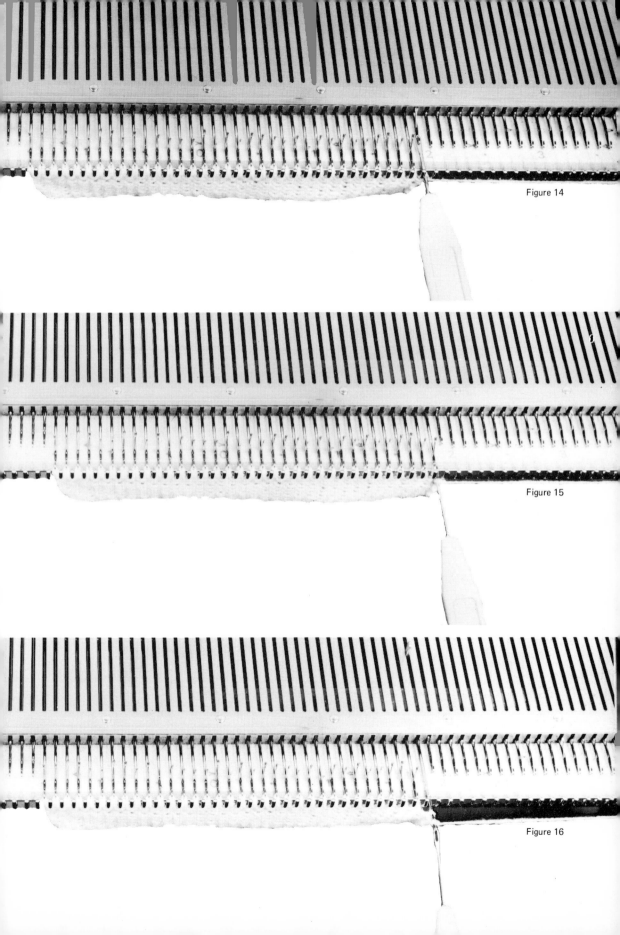

Figure 14

Figure 15

Figure 16

Figure 17

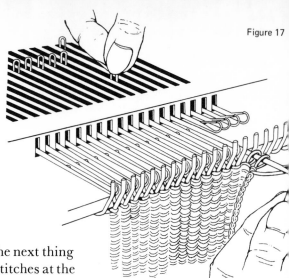

CASTING OFF

If you are knitting your way up a jumper then the next thing you will probably have to do is to cast off a few stitches at the beginning of the armhole shaping. This is why I propose to deal with casting off now and not leave it to the very end as most instruction books do. You always cast off at the side of your work nearest to the carriage.

Transfer one stitch from the end needle to the needle on the left. (This is with the carriage at the right.) Pull the needle with both stitches on it out to D position. Remove your tool from the needle and two stitches are now behind the needle latch. Take your wool and wrap it over the needle (away from the carriage) and inside the latch of the needle (figure 17). Do this with your left hand and with your right hand hold the needle butt and push the needle back to B position. You have simply knitted two stitches together by hand.

Take care not to cast off too tightly. If you have quite a lot of stitches to cast off, then having cast off your first stitch, hook the very end of your work over a sinker post. This will hold the work for you and keep the cast-off stitches even. Casting off is the most tedious job on the machine. There are several other methods, but these will be dealt with as they are needed. The method already described is the most basic and most used. Like all procedures, it becomes easy with practice.

INCREASING

To increase one stitch at either end of your work, simply pull out a new needle to B position and carry on knitting.

When increasing in this way in Fair Isle, lace or a one colour pattern, it is often more satisfactory to increase one stitch at the end of two rows, i.e. the end where the carriage is, rather than at each end of one row. Sometimes in patterning, if the stitch that you have increased is a lace or tuck stitch, or the second colour in Fair Isle, it will miss at the end of the row. By increasing at the beginning of the row you will avoid this.

Fully fashioned increase

This increase method, using your triple eye transfer tool, gives a straight edge to your work, and in this way you are able to sew up your garment to give that more professional finish.

Use the following method to increase one stitch at each end of your work. Using the triple eye transfer tool, transfer the last three stitches out one stitch at each end of your work. You will then be left with an empty needle, being the fourth one in at each end.

If you were to continue knitting now, the empty needle would pick up and knit, but you would be left with a hole under that third needle in. To avoid this, take the bar of the stitch below the fifth needle in and hook it on to the empty fourth needle (figure 18). This will fill in the gap and give you a neat increase.

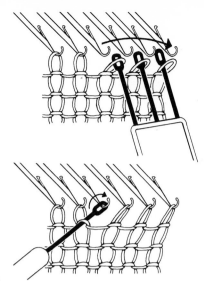

Figure 18

Several increases

The method for casting on several stitches at a time utilizes the hand cast on method, e.g. to increase ten stitches at the beginning of the next two rows. You must increase the stitches at the end where the carriage is because you will need the wool to make the stitches. Bring out ten needles to D position, and starting with the needle nearest your garment, cast on by hand ten stitches using the hand cast on method, winding the wool round the needles in an anti-clockwise direction (figure 19). Check that you have not distorted your aerial tension and knit slowly across from right to left.

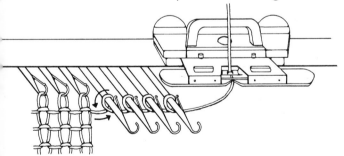

Figure 19

Repeat this procedure, but winding in a clockwise direction, before knitting the next row, but remember to hold the nylon cord over the first lot of ten needles, and the same with the second lot of ten needles on the next row. This is the same method you would use in the hand cast on.

After holding the cord over for a couple of rows, the brush assembly is able to take purchase on the work and you can carry on knitting.

Note: Although a fully fashioned increase takes a little longer than a simple increase, the end results are well worth that little extra trouble, particularly when knitting a plain garment. A knitting pattern usually says whether or not you should employ fully fashioned shaping.

DECREASING

This is a simple procedure with no hidden snags. To decrease one stitch at either end of the garment, transfer the end stitch to the next needle and push the empty needle back to A position. The two stitches on the end needle will knit together and you have a decrease.

If the knitting pattern tells you to decrease fully fashioned, then you use your double or triple eye transfer tool (figure 20). Transfer the three stitches at the end of your work in one stitch, so that you now have two needles with one stitch on each and the third needle in now holds two stitches (A hand knitting pattern would read: Knit 2, knit 2 together). Push the empty needle at the end back to A position. Repeat this procedure at the other end of your work and knit across.

It is possible to do a fully fashioned decreasing as many as five stitches in and achieve a really nice fashioned effect, particularly with raglan shaping.

Useful time savers: If a raglan shaping tells you to decrease one stitch at each end of every other row, it is quicker and looks nicer if you decrease two stitches at the end of every fourth row. Using the triple eye tool, transfer the three end stitches two stitches in, leaving you with one needle with one stitch on and two needles with two stitches on. Push the two empty needles back to A position.

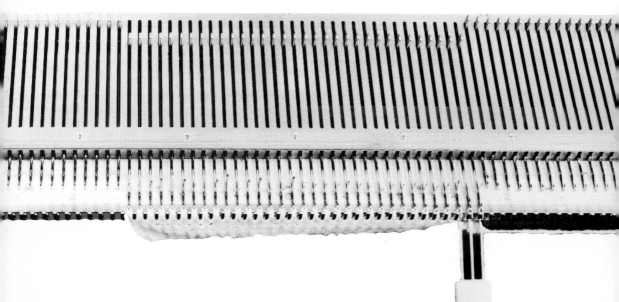

Figure 20

Chapter 5

ROUND NECK SHAPING

The ways of knitting a round neck are many and various and mostly it is a matter of personal preference based on experience. I propose to outline what I think is the easiest method for a beginner, and you can follow your instruction manual and the various knitting patterns to explore the other methods yourself.

A round neck in plain knitting

When you reach the part where the pattern tells you to divide for the neck, it usually says: Hold 30 stitches at the left, cast off 10 stitches in the centre with waste thread (yarn) and work on the first 30 stitches to shape the right-hand side. First of all it is a waste of time to cast off the centre stitches if you are going to pick them up again to knit the neck, so, hold forty stitches at the left in D position (figure 21). Put your front levers to I and shape the neck as per the pattern. If you are decreasing at the neck edge every row or every other row, you can simply put more needles into the holding position instead of casting off or decreasing them. If the shaping at the neck edge is less than every other row say every fourth row, then you must decrease. You cannot hold the stitches, as the gap between the held stitches would be too big and it would pull the neck shaping tight.

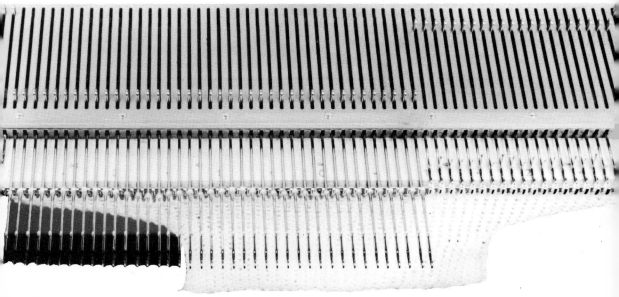

Figure 21

Figure 22

When you have finished the shaping, push thirty needles at the left to C position and shape the left to match the right. When the left side is fiinished, you will be left with your centre shaping stitches out at D position (figure 22). Using the main yarn, put the front levers to II and knit one row across. Run the work off on waste yarn.

Note: As you shape the neck edge, putting the needles into D position, put your wool under the end needle in D position and over the rest of the needles in D position on the shaping row, e.g. if you are knitting the right half and you have put one needle at the neck edge into D position, knit across from right to left and before you knit back, take the wool under that needle in D position (i.e. the needle nearest the knitting) and over the rest of the needles in D position. This has the effect of stopping a gap appearing in between the shaping.

Whenever during the knitting of a garment you are working on a piece that you know you will have to pick up again, try, whenever possible, to run your work off on to waste yarn. It is so much easier to pick up again because the stitches are easily discernible. Using waste yarn is easier than taking your work off on to a knitting needle or holding pin.

'V' NECK SHAPING IN PLAIN KNITTING
Quite often in 'V' shaping, the centre stitch is transferred to the next needle, leaving one empty needle in the centre. Half the work is held at D position (front levers on I), while the right half is shaped as per the pattern. To return the work at the left to the knitting position, put your front levers to II and carry on knitting, shaping the left to match the right.

Neck shaping in pattern is dealt with in chapter 7.

SHOULDER SHAPING

Most shoulder shapings are done by casting off a certain number of stitches at the beginning of alternate rows, so the pattern would read something like: Cast off 6 stitches at the beginning of the next row, knit one row, cast off 6 stitches at the beginning of the next row, knit one row, cast off the remaining 9 stitches. To finish the garment the shoulder seams have to be sewn together and can be quite bulky.

A better method of shaping the shoulders would read as follows: With front levers on I, knit one row from right to left (this is for a right shoulder), put six stitches at the right to D position, knit back to the right. Put your wool under the first needle at the left in D position and then back across all the needles in D position and knit back to the left (figure 23). Put the next six needles into D position at the right and knit to the right. Put the wool under the end needle in D position, over the rest and knit to the left. Put the front levers on II and knit one row from left to right on all needles. Run the shoulder off on to waste yarn.

Note: When shaping the left shoulder remember to reverse the shaping.

When you are ready to join the shoulder seams, put two 'right' shoulders back on to the machine together with the right sides facing each other. You now have two shoulders hooked up on the same set of needles. The first one to be hooked on has the right side facing you, the second one to be hooked on has the wrong side facing you. Knit one row across at tension 10 and cast off using your latchet tool. Shoulders can alternatively be run off on waste thread and grafted together.

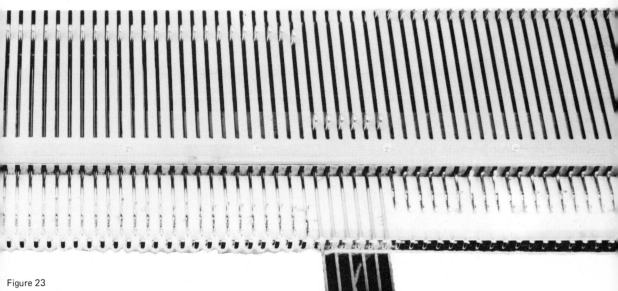

Figure 23

CASTING OFF WITH THE LATCHET TOOL

The latchet tool looks like one of the machine needles on a handle. To cast off with this tool, start from the left of your work, and put the tool through the first stitch. Hook the stitch on to the tool and off the needle. Slip it behind the latch of the tool and transfer the next stitch on to the latchet tool but inside the latch. Slide the first stitch over the second by pulling the tool towards you and closing the latch (figure 24). You are really crocheting the stitches through each other.

You need to hold the work firmly with your left hand as you go along.

This method of casting off is probably the most awkward to master, but is the quickest once mastered. It is also a nice loose cast off that doesn't distort your work. For an even looser cast off, you can take your wool along the row as you cast off and crochet a chain between each cast-off stitch.

For shaping the shoulders in pattern, refer to Chapter 7.

Before casting off with the latchet tool you must always knit one row across at tension 10. This method is only for casting off and not for shaping. It is also only suitable for 4-ply or finer yarns, not for double knitting wool.

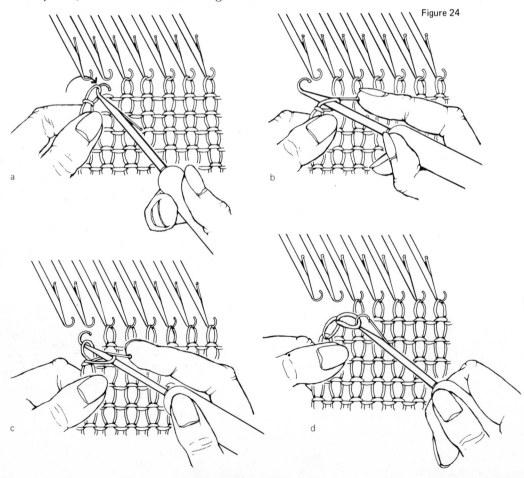

Figure 24

Chapter 6

POCKETS

There are three basic ways of knitting pockets, and each method has its place in machine knitting.

Method one This is a simple patch pocket and is just a square knitted to the size you require and sewn on to the finished garment in the position you require.

Method two Here the pocket is knitted into the garment: First of all, because you are going to hold some needles, move your front levers to I. Decide where your pocket is going to be. If, for example, it is going to be over the centre twenty stitches, then with your carriage at the right, put all the needles to the left of the twenty pocket needles to D position and knit from right to left. Put all the needles to the right of the pocket needles to D position and knit back. You are now knitting on the centre twenty needles (figure 25). Knit the number of rows you require for the depth of the pocket. If you want a pocket twenty rows deep you need to knit forty rows. To put the held needles back, with your carriage to the right, put the needles at the left of the pocket to C position and knit from right to left. Put your front levers to II and carry on knitting on all the needles.

Figure 25

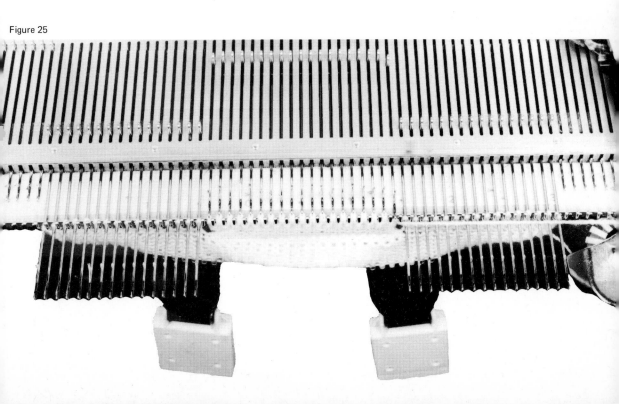

When you are knitting this pocket, you will probably find it useful to attach a weight to the pocket as you knit, as it tends to double up and catch on the brushes. The alternative is to hold the pocket down with your hand.

Remember, if you are counting the rows for a front, for example, then knitting the pocket will add a lot of rows to your row counter. To allow for this, either stop your row counter or adjust it accordingly when your pocket is finished.

When your garment is complete, all you have to do is press the pocket well and sew up the side seams.

Method three This method is possibly one of the most widely used. It is quick, easy and gives a nice flat pocket.

When you reach the row where the pocket is to be, bring out the needles required for the width of the pocket to D position. Taking a length of waste yarn, knit the needles back to B position. This is achieved by anchoring your waste yarn to the first needle and then placing the yarn over each needle in turn, through the latch of the needle and pushing the needle back to B position. Carry on and finish the piece.

After completing your work, press it before embarking on knitting the pocket. With the work right side up and facing you, remove the contrast yarn. You will now have a 'gash' in the knitting the width of the pocket (figure 26). Transfer the open stitches at the bottom of this 'gash' on to the machine

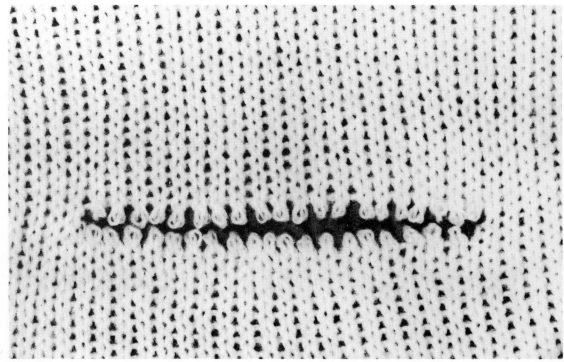

Figure 26

and knit the top edge, e.g. if the edge is to be five stitches deep, knit five rows at your main tension, minus one. Knit one row at tension 10 to make the fold and then another five rows at the preceding tension. Run the hem off on waste yarn and this can be sewn down later on the right side using a running backstitch, explained in Chapter 10.

To knit the back and depth of the pocket, again with the right side facing you, hook the second row of open stitches on to the machine and knit the depth you require at the main tension of the garment, and cast off.

The sides of the pocket can be stitched together and sewn to the base of the hem already completed.

Note: If as a beginner you find it tricky to remove the waste yarn before knitting this pocket you can quite easily leave the waste yarn in position until the pocket is completed. In this case it would not be necessary to press the work before knitting the pocket.

DARTS

A dart is a simple but useful procedure used in the shaping of skirts, the backs of trousers or babies' leggings and in shaping ladies' jumpers.

A circular skirt knitted on a machine is simply a series of darts joined by several rows of plain knitting.

Probably the easiest way to describe a dart, is to liken it to a hand knitting pattern. The pattern will probably say: With 30 stitches on the needles, knit 5 stitches and turn, knit 10 stitches and turn etc., thus shaping the work.

To achieve this on your machine, put your front levers to I as stitches are to be held. With, for example, thirty stitches on the machine, put twenty-five needles at the left out to D position and knit across. This will have only knitted on the first five needles in B position. Before moving the carriage back to the right, hook the wool under the end right-hand needle in D position and over the remainder of those needles, then knit back to the right. Push five needles (or however many the pattern says) back to C position and knit to the left. Continue repeating this procedure until all the needles are back in B position, remembering at the end of each row to the left to hook the wool under the end needle in D position and over the rest (see instructions for shoulder shaping). Once all the needles are back in B position, normal knitting is continued until the next dart is required.

BUTTONHOLES

For a small buttonhole suitable for a child's garment, transfer one stitch to its adjacent needle and carry on knitting. The machine will pick up and knit on the empty needle, leaving a small hole for the buttonhole.

Most button bands are knitted double on the machine, therefore two holes will be needed for each buttonhole. You can, when the garment is completed, buttonhole round to join the edges of the buttonhole together but be careful not to make it too small in doing so.

For a larger buttonhole, make the 'hole' over two needles by hooking one stitch to the needle to its left and one to the needle to the right. This will leave two empty needles in B position. Knit two rows. As the machine will not successfully pick up what is in effect two dropped stitches, pick up one of the loops and transfer it to one of the two needles forming the buttonhole, and carry on knitting.

To knit a large buttonhole

For a buttonhole of any size, usually three or more stitches wide, the same principle is used as with the third pocket method. Decide where you want your buttonhole to be and knit those stitches by hand with a piece of contrast thread and then continue knitting. When your garment is complete make sure that you press it well over the buttonholes and then carefully remove the contrast thread and seal the two edges of the buttonhole by grafting.

Note: When removing contrast thread from your work it is easier to snip the thread in several places with a pair of small scissors and remove it in several pieces rather than pulling it out in one long piece.

Another buttonhole

Having picked up your button band, for a band twenty rows wide in all proceed as follows: Knit five rows and mark the needles that are to be your buttonholes by pulling them out to D position and knitting them back to B position using waste thread (figure 27). Knit five rows and one row at tension 10. Knit another five rows. Bring the first set of buttonhole needles on the right slightly forwards. With your transfer tool pick up the first loop from the right of the first row knitted after the waste yarn and hook it on to the first buttonhole needle (figure 28). Knit it in. ('Knit it in' means knit back by hand, not with carriage.)

Transfer the second stitch on to the first needle and knit (figure 29). Return the first stitch on to the second needle leaving your first needle empty.

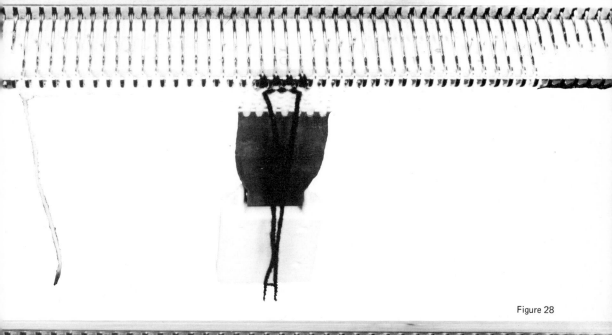

Figure 27

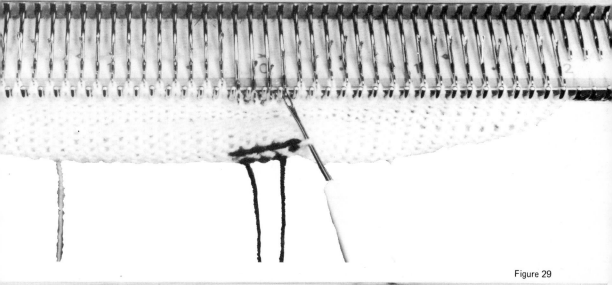

Figure 28

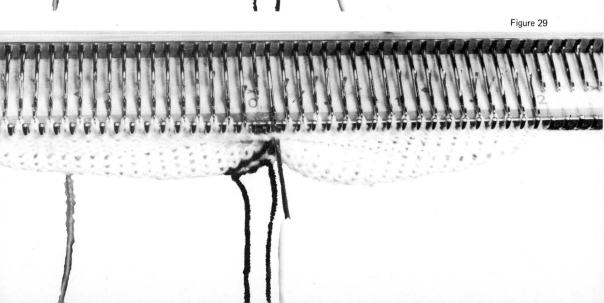

Figure 29

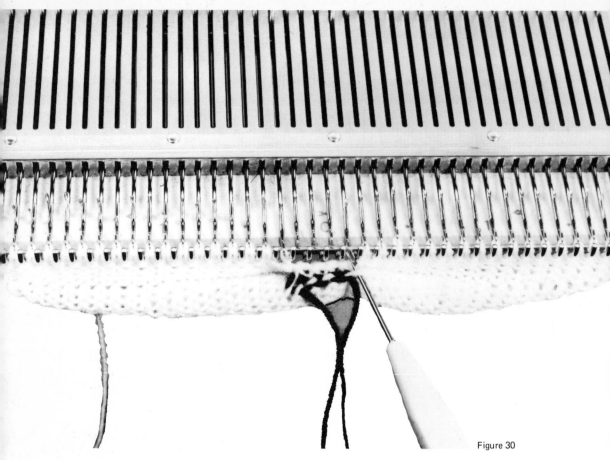

Figure 30

Pick up the second stitch after the waste yarn, place it on to
the second needle and knit it. Transfer the third stitch from
the third needle on to the second needle and knit it. Continue
in this way until all the stitches after the waste yarn are
picked up and knitted. Also pick up one stitch at the end
beyond the waste yarn to avoid a hole.

Transfer the second row of stitches after the waste yarn on to
the empty needles (figure 30). Pull out the waste yarn when
you have completed the buttonholes and knit five rows. This
buttonhole is the neatest and gives a garment that
professional finish. It is much harder to describe than it is to
knit.

Girl's short sleeve
jumper and circular
skirt (page 76)

Lady's overtop (page 70)

Stockings (page 78)

Child's ha[...]
scarf and jump[...]
(pages 73 and 7[...]

Fair Isle samplers

Fair Isle samplers

Children's tank tops
(page 75)

Lady's round neck
jumper and man's
'V' neck sweater
(pages 68 and 72)

Fair Isle samplers

Lady's tabard
(page 71)

Fair Isle samplers

BUTTON AND BUTTONHOLE BANDS

On a single bed machine button and buttonhole bands are either knitted lengthways and then sewn on to the garment or the work is turned sideways and the band is picked up and knitted on to the garment. Both methods are satisfactory and it is mostly a question of personal choice.

To knit a band lengthways

If the pattern does not tell you how many rows to knit for the bands then it is up to you to measure the garment and decide for yourself roughly how long the band needs to be. It should be long enough to fit the garment with the band slightly stretched. Always knit a few more rows than you think you will need: it only takes seconds to unravel extra rows; it takes longer to pick up the stitches and knit more rows if you are short. Do not cast the band off, leave it on waste thread then you can make the adjustment to the length easily if necessary.

To knit a band sideways

If the band is knitted sideways you will probably have to pick up your stitches in two sections. Usually you will pick up the stitches along one front, the top of a sleeve and to the centre of the back of the neck. You then repeat the process along the other front, across the top of the second sleeve and again to the centre of the back of the neck. This will leave you with just one seam at the back of the neck.

On a long jacket you may have to pick up the bands in three sections in which case you would pick up each front separately and then the third piece would be across one sleeve top, the back of the neck and across the top of the other sleeve.

There are two ways of picking up the bands:

Method one
With the wrong side of the work facing you, pick the stitches up evenly along the garment edge. If the pattern does not indicate how many stitches you need to pick up then gauge it as follows: Hold your edge to be picked up against the machine and stretch it slightly but do not pull it tight. Centre the work so that you are picking up the same number of stitches at each side of 0. Put the end three stitches at the right and left edges of the work on to the machine and then put the middle three stitches on. Now work across from right to left putting on every tenth stitch. Once you have got every tenth stitch on the machine, fill in picking up every stitch. This method will ensure that you pick up your stitches evenly across the work.

When picking up stitches for a band you must not pick up the edge stitch. Go down one row and pick up the whole stitch, not just one bar of the stitch. Keep to the row that you start so that your band is even and picked up in a straight line.

Bands knitted in this way are always knitted double so remember to do the centre row at four tensions looser to give you a fold line. When you have knitted the number of rows required for the band pick up every other stitch from the first row of the band and put them on to alternate needles along the length of the band.

Knit one row across at tension 10 and cast off loosely using your latchet tool. Your band is complete and you have no sewing to do.

Method two
With the right side of the work facing you pick up the required number of stitches using the same principles as described in method one. Knit the band but instead of picking up the first row and casting off you need to knit two extra rows and then run the work off on waste yarn. The two extra rows are to ensure that when the band is sewn down afterwards it will overlap the pick-up row and give a neat edge.

To finish off this band it is sewn down on the right side using a running backstitch described in Chapter 10.

NECKBANDS
To knit a round neckband
If the garment has a set-in sleeve, then before knitting the neckband you must join one shoulder seam.

The stitches are picked up evenly along the front of the neck and across the back of the neck.

Alternatively, if the garment has raglan sleeves you are usually instructed by the pattern to join three raglan seams and then pick up the stitches across the top of one sleeve, round the front neck, across the top of the other sleeve and across the back neck. It is not necessary to join the raglan seams before picking up the work on the machine. It is quite in order to pick up the pieces separately and put them on to the machine but do take care that you put them on in the right order.

Both the methods described in the button band section can be applied to the neckbands but these methods are usually more suitable for a 'V' neck rather than a round neck. Round neckbands are usually knitted in welt. To knit a neckband in 2 x 1 or 1 x 1 welt etc., first of all pick up every stitch as previously described. Knit one row and then transfer your stitches for the type of welt required. This first row before you transfer the stitches should be knitted at the main tension.

If you are using the first method with the wrong side facing you then you will pick up the first row on every other needle, knit one row at tension 10 and cast off loosely with your latchet tool. It is a good idea to do one chain between each cast-off stitch to give a really loose cast off.

If you are using the second method, with the right side of the work facing you, then knit the band as follows: For a band ten rows deep, pick up your stitches (do not count this row), transfer the stitches for welt, tension dial at rib tension, knit ten rows, knit one row at tension 10, nine rows at rib tension and then bring all the needles into the working position and knit a further three rows. Run the work off on waste thread.

'V' neckbands

The two front pieces of the neckband are knitted separately and the back of the neck is either knitted on its own or together with one of the front pieces.

All the same principles apply to 'V' neckbands as for round necks. To mitre the centre of the 'V' neckband work as follows: For a band twenty-two rows in all, knit eleven rows decreasing at the neck edge of the second and every alternate row for eleven rows, and then knit eleven rows increasing at the neck edge on the second and every alternate row.

To knit a 'V' neck without the mitred centre simply knit straight and the edges are then overlapped and sewn down.

Note: When you have picked up the stitches for a 'V' neckband, bring out an extra needle at the 'V' neck edge to B position, thus increasing one stitch when you knit the first row. This gives you an extra stitch for sewing up purposes.

Chapter 7

PATTERN CARDS FOR PUNCHCARD MACHINES

The pattern cards for semi-automatic machines such as the Knitmaster 302 are quite straightforward instruction cards and need no special explanation. The pattern cards I am dealing with in this section are the punchcards used with the Knitmaster 321, 323 and 326 automatic machines.

Knitting a pattern using the punchcards is as easy as plain knitting: it is only a matter of setting up the machine and observing one or two basic rules. Each pattern card is 24 stitches wide, your instruction manual will tell you how many rows to each complete pattern so far as the basic pattern set is concerned.

To put the card into the machine, open the pattern panel and insert the card with the letter A at the bottom right-hand side (figure 31). If the card is one that you have punched out yourself then instead of the letter A at the bottom right-hand side it will have the number of your machine, e.g. 321. Feed the card in slowly by turning the feeding dial and using the clips (small green buttons) provided. Clip the card into a drum so that it will rotate continually. Turn the card until row 1 shows in the pattern panel and lock the card by closing the pattern panel.

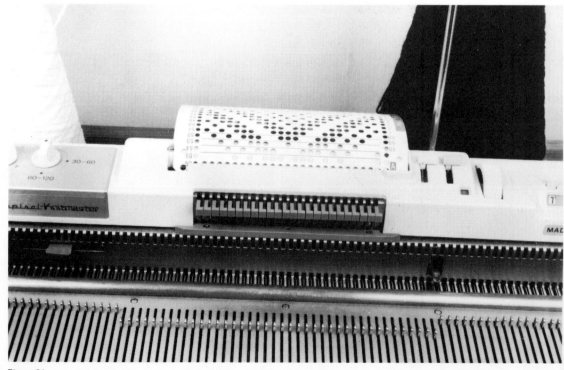

Figure 31

t is most important that you should realize that the machine will *not* knit the pattern until the carriage has passed the pattern panel at least once. The pattern is then fed into the memory banks and it will take up the pattern. Therefore if you insert your card right at the beginning of your garment and lock it on row one then the pattern is being fed into the memory banks whilst you are knitting your hem etc.

If for some reason you want to read the pattern into the carriage without knitting the row put the side levers forwards (towards you), set the cam lever to S for slip and you can take the carriage across the work without knitting.

Note: If at this point you have any needles in the holding position remember to check that the front levers are at I.

Once the hem is knitted and you are ready to knit the pattern, release the stop knob on the pattern panel so that the card will rotate and set the cam lever to the appropriate letter, e.g. F for Fair Isle. Remember that if you are knitting Fair Isle you must thread up with your second colour.

Always remember that to knit the pattern correctly the carriage *must* pass the whole of the pattern panel each time you knit a row. It is easy to forget about this when you have only a few stitches on the machine. Failure to pass the pattern panel results in a broken pattern or no pattern at all.

NECK SHAPING IN PATTERN

When shaping a neck in pattern the first thing you must do is to make a note of the number showing in the pattern panel at the point where you want to divide for the neck. Write it down — if you don't you will forget it and you need to know the number so that you can return the card to the same position when you knit the other half of the neck.

The main difference between neck shaping in plain knitting and neck shaping when knitting a pattern lies in the way in which you hold the stitches. It is possible to hold the stitches out at D position as for plain knitting but when you want to return them to the knitting position you must put them back by hand using the transfer tool. You cannot return them by pushing the needles back to C position — the pattern will not be knitted for one row.

The best way to hold stitches when knitting in pattern is as follows: Bring the needles to be held out to D position and then using your nylon cord or a piece of waste thread knit the stitches on these needles right back to A position. When the shaping is finished you can return the needles to the working position simply by unravelling the nylon cord or thread.

Having knitted the right half of the neck, *before* you return the left half of the stitches to the working position, turn the pattern card to the number that was showing when you divided for the neck, lock the pattern panel and take the carriage across the panel. The correct row is now ready to be knitted. Unravel the nylon cord, release the pattern card, set the cam lever to the correct letter, make sure that your wool is correctly threaded, and carry on to shape the left side to match the right.

SHOULDER SHAPING IN PATTERN

The shoulders can be shaped by holding stitches instead of casting them off as in plain knitting, the only difference being that before you do one row across all the stitches at the end of the shaping you must return the needles to the knitting position by using the transfer tool. The alternative is to hold the stitches by knitting them back to A position with the nylon cord or waste thread. The last row of the shoulders should be done in plain knitting.

If you make a mistake when knitting in pattern, don't panic, it is not as tragic as it seems at first. If you need to unravel several rows, work to a system. Unravel one row, turn your row counter back one row and turn your pattern card back one row. Work like this until the correct number of rows have been unravelled. When you have finished unravelling, lock the pattern card and take the carriage across the work without knitting (side levers forwards, cam lever on S for slip). The correct row is now in the carriage and you can continue knitting. Check that you have got the machine threaded correctly with the aerial tension as it should be.

There are three main points to remember when using pattern cards:

1 You must preset the first row by taking the carriage past the pattern panel at least once.

2 Always ensure that you take the carriage completely past the pattern panel on every row.

3 When dividing for a neck make a note of the number showing in the pattern panel.

Chapter 8

SINGLE MOTIF KNITTING

Single motif knitting can be great fun, it is creative and allows plenty of scope for experimenting with your knitting. The biggest mistake, however, is made by the beginner who insists on trying the single motif knitting before she has mastered the basic techniques.

Single motif knitting is not difficult but you need to have confidence in your machine. It is a chore to be constantly referring to your instruction book for basic procedures as well as trying something new. Get confidence in your machine, master the basic techniques and then you will enjoy motif knitting.

Motif knitting is a special feature of the Knitmaster 323 machine, it being possible to knit a single motif automatically on this machine. It is a quite simple procedure, however, to knit a single motif on the 321 machine by selecting the needles manually.

To knit a single motif on the 321

To knit a single motif on the 321 the card must be punched in reverse. The holes must be punched where the white shows through and not the black.

When the card is punched, insert it with 321 at the bottom right and lock it on row one. Set the tension dial to approximately 6, side levers back ▲, front levers on II, and arm lever on 0.

Use two different colours of 4-ply yarn and thread colour one into feeder one and make a hand cast on over fifty needles. Knit several rows and finish with the carriage at the right. Remove colour one from feeder one and thread colour two into feeder one. Thread colour one into feeder two. Release the card and set the cam lever to F for Fair Isle.

1. Bring all but the centre 24 needles to D position; as a guide there is a ◇ between needles 12 and 13 at each side of the centre. The 24 needles are the width of one pattern. Bring the yarn of colour two under the first needle in D position at the left of the needles in B position and over the other needles in D position. Knit from left to right.

2. Bring all except the centre 24 needles to D position, bring the thread of colour two under the first needle in D position at the left of the needles in B position and over the other needles in B position. Knit from left to right.

Repeat these two procedures until 1 is showing in your pattern panel. Your motif is then complete. Rethread colour one into feeder one, remove colour two, remove the card and set the cam lever to 0 for plain knitting and continue knitting.

Single motif knitting on the 323
To knit a single motif on the 323 the pattern cards are punched out normally. Use good quality 4-ply yarn, no thicker. You cannot knit a single motif using yarn that requires a tension higher than tension 7. For the best results use yarns of the same ply and type. Insert your card in the usual way and lock it on row one. If for example you have been knitting in the main colour then before you begin to knit your single motif you must put on the motif attachments.

The needle bed is marked every twenty-fourth needle with a ◇ and this is the width of a complete pattern. Half a pattern is indicated by an X.

Decide where you want your motif to be: for a complete pattern it can be anywhere on your knitting so long as it is between two ◇ s. Insert the motif plate behind the butts of the 24 needles that are to be your motif. Place the plate with the raised edge to the rear of the machine. Attach the two grey plastic motif cams to the carriage, behind the side levers (figure 32). To do this it is necessary to bring the side levers forwards and then set them back again.

Take two thread separators and place them underneath a group of three needles being the fourth, fifth and sixth needles away from each edge of your knitting, i.e. go to the edge of your knitting, count three empty needles and then put the separators under the next three needles.

Put the main colour yarn running on top of the thread

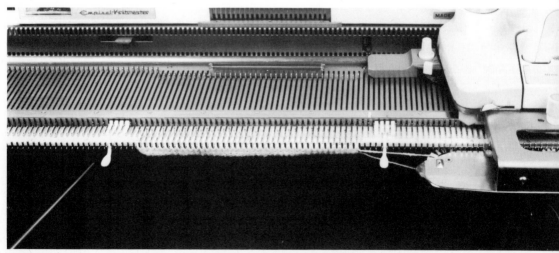

Figure 32

separators and thread up with colour two in feeder two and let the second colour run underneath the separators.

Set the cam lever to F for Fair Isle, release the pattern card and knit from right to left. To get a neat edge to your motif, after knitting each row take the thread in feeder two and wrap it once round the first needle in the main colour, i.e. the first needle next to the last stitch of motif knitting.

When your motif is complete remove all attachments and the pattern card and colour two, set the machine for plain knitting and carry on.

To knit a single motif on the 326

To knit a single motif on the 326 machine the basic procedures are as for the 323.

To determine the position of the motif, two plastic pieces are placed on the needle bed over the required number of needles, e.g. 24 for one complete motif. These pieces differ from the metal plates used on the 323 in that they can be moved closer together or further apart as you please. Therefore to knit a motif over twelve needles the plastic pieces (point cams) can be placed twelve needles apart. These point cams are coloured, the left one being yellow and the right one red.

The grey plastic cams are attached to the carriage as for the 323, the only difference being that they are slightly larger than those on the 323 (figure 33).

On the pattern panel of the 326, next to the card stop knob is a yellow knob marked L and S. When the knob is on S the card knits in the normal way but when the knob is switched to L the card only moves round on alternate rows and so the length of the card is doubled.

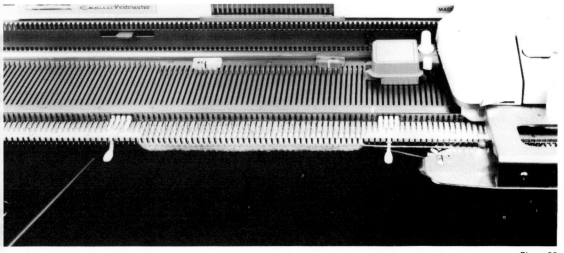

Figure 33

The main point to watch as you knit a single motif is that the main colour stays on top of the separators and the contrast colour runs underneath. If you make a mistake, unravel the knitting in the usual way. Don't forget to turn back your card and reset the row. Knit your single motif slowly and carefully and you will have no trouble. You may find it a help to insert the weaving brushes when knitting a single motif. This is entirely a matter of personal preference. If you do use the brushes remove then them when you have finished the motif.

Once you have gained confidence in your machine and have knitted several single motifs you will want to try more advanced techniques. It is possible to use up to seven motif plates at once and by adding and removing plates and using different cards many exciting designs can be produced.

The motif plates can be used in groups to 'cut off' the pattern so that you are knitting a complete pattern instead of, say, two and a half patterns. For example, if you want to knit roses along the bottom of a lady's cardigan and the number of stitches to be cast on is one hundred, you will have three complete roses and then two half roses at each side. By using the motif attachments and three motif plates you can knit the three complete roses and omit the two half patterns. The procedure is exactly the same as knitting a single motif except that you are using three motif plates instead of one.

Single motifs can also be knitted in punch lace and weaving but in each case the end needle must be brought out to D position at the beginning of each row. Tuck stitch and slip stitch cannot be used for motif knitting.

Chapter 9

PUNCHING PATTERNS

Each pattern is 24 stitches wide and a full card is 60 rows.

When punching a pattern card begin punching on the row immediately above the second perforated row from the bottom of the card. If the pattern is less than 60 rows, e.g. 32 rows, then punch out rows 33 and 34 and cut off the upper portion of the card.

To make the fastening of the card easy, cut in slightly both ends of the top of the card as on the bottom. Finally, punch two holes either side for fastening. Pattern cards of 40 rows or more rotate more easily than cards of less than 40 rows.

First of all, punch out the guide holes at each corner of the paper pattern. Punch them out as accurately as possible. Hold the paper pattern with *top* pointing upwards. Hold the card so that the number of your machine, e.g. 326, is facing you in the top left-hand corner.

Put the plastic card on top of the paper pattern and clip them together with your green plastic buttons or secure them with paper clips. The black dots on the paper pattern show through the holes of the plastic card and these are to be punched out. You can either punch through both the card and the pattern or you can use a chinagraph pencil and mark the card on the holes needing to be punched. The paper pattern can then be removed and the holes punched through the card only. This second method is easier on the hands for punching and keeps your pattern intact for further use.

Punch the card by holding it sideways and start from the bottom. The punch only reaches half the width of the card so you must punch one half and then turn your card.

When punching, make sure that the pilot pin on your punch is centred in the small hole already punched in the plastic card. This will ensure that the hole you punch will be central.

If you make a mistake and punch a hole in the wrong place, cover the mistake on *both* sides of the card with Sellotape and repunch correctly.

Remember that row one showing on the row indicator when the pattern is inserted in the machine is row six counting from the bottom of the card.

PATTERN INFORMATION
Slip stitch (figure 34)
The slip stitch patterns knit with the pattern side facing you as you knit. The slip stitch is formed by the yarn remaining in front of the knitted fabric instead of knitting. Slip stitch tends to draw the fabric in; it is advisable therefore to knit at least one full tension higher than for stockinet.

Tuck stitch (figure 35)
Tuck stitch patterns are very effective particularly when knitted in fine yarns. They do, however, need careful measuring for the correct tension but the end results are well worth any extra effort.

Tuck stitch patterns are very effective, particularly when some of the tuck stitch patterns are equally attractive on either side. Tuck stitch tends to knit up much tighter than plain knitting but it keeps its width. The effect is that you will have a short, fat piece of knitting in comparison to the same piece knitted in stockinet.

It is advisable, especially for beginners, to knit a tuck stitch garment using a tuck stitch pattern otherwise careful adjustments must be made to obtain the correct measurements.

Two colour tuck stitch (figure 36)
These patterns are a tuck stitch but the colour of yarn is changed in feeder one as indicated. Two colours cannot be knitted together as in Fair Isle. Two colour tuck stitch patterns knit with the wrong side of the work facing you. An effective raised pattern is achieved, ideal for border patterns.

Note: If the pattern is four rows long, you will be changing colour every fourth row. Make sure that you start the card on row one otherwise your pattern will not be correct. On the Knitmaster 323 machine the tuck stitch brushes are attached for tuck stitch only. Other machines are set as per instructions for tucking.

Fair Isle (figure 37)
Fair Isle is knitted with the main yarn in feeder one and the second colour in feeder two. Sometimes the yarns are reversed to give the desired effect. Check with your pattern book, this will tell you.

For the best results two yarns of the same type and ply should be used except where you are trying to produce a particular effect, e.g. black wool with a gold lurex thread. Usually in Fair Isle knitting the tension dial needs to be one full tension higher than for plain knitting.

Figure 34   Figure 35

Figure 36   Figure 37

The Fair Isle knits with the wrong side of the work facing you. When you are knitting a Fair Isle pattern with long floats at the back, i.e. a large pattern, it is advisable to bring the first needle at the beginning of each row to D position. This will prevent your second colour from tangling round the brushes.

Punch lace (figure 38)

A lace effect is achieved by knitting a transparent thread in feeder two. This thread can be obtained from most machine stockists. When knitting with this type of thread always knit one row with both the yarn and the transparent thread in feeder one. This is to anchor the thread before you start the lace knitting.

Transfer the fine thread from feeder one to feeder two, set the cam lever to L for lace and release your pattern card. You may find it necessary to wind the fine thread twice round the aerial tension wheel in order to get sufficient tension.

Punch lace knits up with the wrong side of the work facing you and generally knits at the same tension as plain knitting.

Figure 38

Attractive patterns can be achieved by substituting cotton or a lurex thread for the transparent thread so this is an area for experimentation.

If you are knitting cotton from a reel, secure the reel by slotting it over a projection of some kind. A six-inch nail hammered into a square of wood will suffice. This will stop your cotton from rolling about and causing troubles.

Plaiting

A feature of the 326 model is the plaiting stitch. This stitch can only be done on stocking stitch or tuck stitch. A second colour in a fine yarn is threaded through the back of the feeder behind the main yarn and this thread is plaited over the main yarn. The effect of this pattern is to give a two colour fabric which in many cases is reversible.

WEAVING (figure 39)

Weaving is probably the most attractive feature of a knitting machine. This is because it is possible to use such a wide variety of yarns and therefore produce many different results.

The background yarn, i.e. the yarn actually knitted, should be a soft 4-ply or finer. Nothing should be used that requires a tension higher than tension 7 otherwise the fabric will be too hard. Any yarn can be used for the actual weaving. Rug wool, blanket wool and thick tweed wools all produce interesting and very hardwearing fabrics.

Figure 39

To weave

Insert the weaving brushes by loosening the thumb screws on the carriage brush unit and slotting the brushes under the screws, *behind* the yarn. Tighten up the thumb screws. Having preset your pattern card the cam lever stays on centre 0 for stockinet. Thread the weaving yarn through the second yarn brake and bring it down in front of the knitting thread. With the carriage at the right put the weaving thread inside the left-hand weaving guide — the small red knob projecting from the top of the brush assembly (figure 40). Attach the yarn to your machine clamp to secure it. At the beginning of each row bring the first needle out to D position. The side levers are back, front levers on II and cam lever on 0. Knit slowly to the left. Remove the weaving yarn from the left-hand guide pin, pull it down well to clear the brushes and hook it inside the right-hand guide pin. Bring the first needle at the left to D position and knit to the right.

As you knit across it is a good idea to allow the weaving thread to run *loosely* through the fingers of your left hand. This will keep the thread at a constant tension because you tend to disturb the tension as you remove the yarn from one pin to transfer it across. Do *not* hang on to the yarn but allow it to run freely.

Although lengths of material can be woven and then cut to shape and sewn it is very easy and more economical to shape the garment on the machine. Woven garments are warm, hard wearing and quite economical on wool. It is difficult to calculate how much weaving yarn you will need to each ball of knitting yarn. The nearest guide that I can find is, assuming that both balls of yarn are the same weight, one ball of weaving yarn to two balls of knitting yarn. Weaving is ideal for all kinds of soft furnishings and is a tremendous money saver in this respect. Chair coverings, cushion covers,

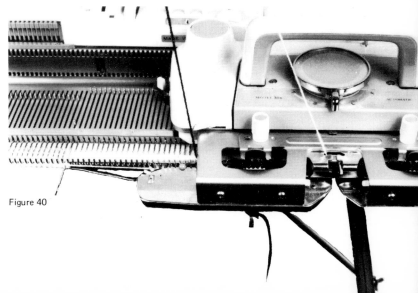

Figure 40

lampshades and rugs are just a few of the things that you can produce for your home at a fraction of the cost of shop products.

To practise your weaving make small items such as pencil cases, oven gloves or jazzy tote bags for the children. You will be pleased and encouraged with the results.

A tension square in weaving is easily knitted in the usual way and measured on the wrong side of the work. Weaving is produced with the pattern side facing you as you knit and as there is very little 'give' in weaving it is quite easy to measure the work on the machine.

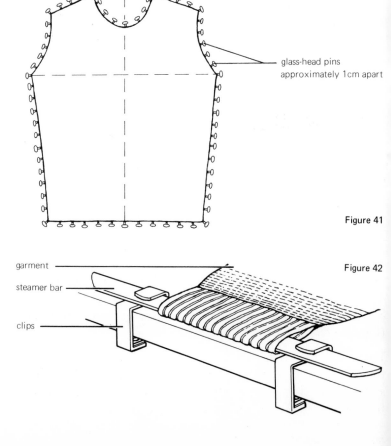

glass-head pins
approximately 1cm apart

Figure 41

garment

steamer bar

clips

Figure 42

56

Chapter 10

GARMENT FINISHING

Having spent quite some time and space in this book on the preparation necessary before one starts to knit a garment it is equally important that as much time is spent on the careful finishing of that same garment. As you become more experienced in machine knitting you will realize that the actual knitting is only a small part of producing the garment. The secret of success lies in the preparation and finishing.

Once the garment is finished the first job is to sew in all the ends neatly. *Never* join your yarn in the middle of a row, always at the end. Use a wool needle and sew the ends in by neatly weaving them into the back of your work. Snip them off. When you do join in a new ball of wool leave yourself a long enough end to darn in easily.

The next task is to block and press the garment pieces. I can almost hear the groans as you read this, but garment pressing, although time consuming, is not difficult and it is essential if you want that professional finish.

Use a firm, flat surface (your ironing board is not big enough). A piece of Essex board or something of that nature can be easily obtained from your local wood shop and is not expensive. Use glass-head pins for blocking your work; they are slightly more expensive than ordinary pins but much easier to handle on woollen garments (figure 41). Cover your pressing surface with a piece of old sheeting or cloth and secure it.

Pin out each piece carefully to size. Check the measurements as you go. First of all pin out the four corners and then fill in putting in pins about every cm. Pin the garment with wrong side facing you.

Read the manufacturer's instructions for pressing the yarn if there are any available. Generally a pure wool needs a wet cloth and a hot iron. Press the work smoothly: don't bang your iron up and down and leave a trail of iron marks. Acrylics need a dry cloth and warm iron. Acrylics can be easily ruined by over-pressing so take care.
Steam the welts and cuffs by using the steamer bar provided (figure 42).

Put the clips on to the edge of your pressing board and insert the steamer bar through the welt of your knitting. Clip the steamer bar into the two clips and pull the knitting away from you until the rib stitches are closed up and the knitting is gathered. This is done with the wrong side of the knitting uppermost. Put the pressing cloth over the welt and then allow the heat from the iron to penetrate the knitting. *Do not* put the iron on to the cloth.

Sewing up

There are quite a number of different ways to sew up a knitted garment. Mostly it is a case of personal choice, but certainly you should *never* oversew a garment. Oversewing does not give a strong seam and it shows on the right side of the garment.

Backstitch

Make three small running stitches one on top of the other at the edge of the seam and then put the needle through the beginning of the stitches and pull the yarn through to the back. Insert the needle from the back to the front the length of another small stitch and pull the yarn through. Continue along the seam in this way keeping the stitches small and neat.

This gives a good, firm seam and is quick and easy to do. Check when sewing a Fair Isle pattern that you match the pattern edges carefully. If you are using a backstitch, pin the edges of the garment together first.

When sewing up hems, welts, etc. join the outside seam and then the inside seam: do not sew through four thicknesses at once. To sew a button band on, pin it first so that it is just slightly stretched. Sew round the first edge of the band and then join the two ends. Turn the band in and sew down the inner seam.

Mattress stitch (figure 43)

This is the neatest stitch although it is the most difficult to do. However, a few minutes' practice is all that it takes and once you have mastered it this stitch is quick and neat and pleasant to do. The garment is sewn up on the right side.

You can if you wish pin the pieces every few cm to keep them in line. Using the same colour yarn as your garment take the needle through the crossbars of the first two stitches on the piece on your right. Take the needle across to the piece on the left and through the crossbars of the first two stitches. Repeat this process from right to left, pulling the wool every few stitches so that the edges of the work are pulled together. Do not use the first two stitches at the very edge of the garment piece. Go in one stitch first, and then stick to this row to keep your seam straight.

This seam is virtually invisible on the right side and is particularly suitable for trousers and skirt seams. Mattress

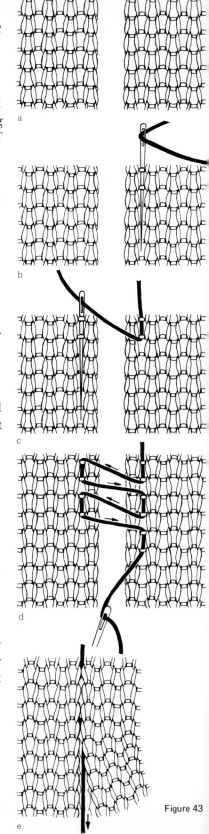

a

b

c

d

e

Figure 43

58

stitch has the added advantage of being worked on the right side and therefore it is a simple matter to match any Fair Isle pattern correctly. Mattress stitch is a must for joining neck, cuff and welt seams.

Machine sewing

Machine sewing causes much controversy in the knitting machine world, but like everything else if it is done correctly it works. Strong thread that will give with the knitting is needed and a machine that does a zigzag stitch. Trousers can be successfully sewn using a straight stitch because they are knitted at a much tighter tension and the fabric is therefore firm.

Backstitch for neckbands and button bands

Having picked up the band on the right side and finished off by running it off on waste yarn you now need to sew the band down on the right side.

First of all you need to pin the band into position making sure that you have covered the pick-up row. Start from the right-hand side and use the yarn that you have used for the neck. Thread up your wool needle and bring it up from behind through the second stitch of the last row knitted. (Leave the waste yarn in place until you have finished sewing.) Then put the needle back into the first stitch, up into the third, back into the second, up into the fourth and so on until you have sewn right across the band going in and out of each stitch, securing it to the garment (figure 44).

Carefully remove the waste yarn, and, before you join the ends together, steam the neck as for the cuffs and welt.

Sewing on buttons

If possible sew the buttons on with wool not with cotton. If the wool is too thick try splitting it. Cotton may cut through the knitting, but, if you have to use it, use a good quality synthetic thread.

Zips

Zips can be a nuisance to manage but the golden rule is to pin them into position first. Do not stretch the knitting and nor should you push the knitting up to fit the zip in. It should be pinned evenly as close to the edge as possible and sewn down with a small neat running stitch. The zip can be sewn down on the right side quite invisibly if you make your sewing stitches by carefully catching the crossbars of the knitted stitches.

Hems

The neatest way to sew down a hem is by using the same method as I have just described for zips. Pin the hem

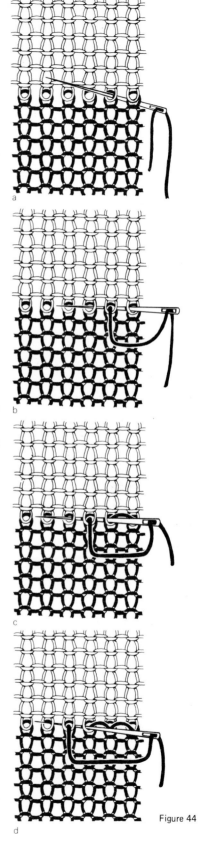

Figure 44

59

carefully and then working on the right side of the garment sew the hem by catching down the crossbars of the stitches. Use matching thread. The alternative is to hem it on the inside using fine wool or thread.

Cuffs, neckbands and welts

Cuffs and welts etc. are usually knitted double and you are therefore faced with four thicknesses to join. *Never* sew through all four thicknesses. Join the outside seam first, preferably with mattress stitch, and then the inside seam.

Trousers and skirts

Mattress stitch is really the ideal way to join trouser and skirt seams but if you don't wish to use this stitch then it must be a neat, firm backstitch. Sew trouser and skirt seams from the bottom upwards.

Note: It is a good idea when you are knitting trousers or skirts to mark each piece as you knit it. This avoids such nasty mistakes as two left legs.

Grafting

Grafting is used to join two lots of open stitches together. Instead of casting off the work is run off on waste thread. Before grafting, press the work to set the open stitches and carefully remove the waste yarn.

A row of false knitting is produced by weaving the sewing thread in and out of the open stitches. You will of course be using the same yarn as the knitted pieces.

To graft two pieces together you must have the same number of stitches on each piece. Use a wool needle (blunt end) and lay the two pieces to be joined edge to edge with the right sides facing (figure 45).

1 Put the needle from the back to the front through the first stitch on the right-hand side of the lower piece.

2 Put the needle into the first loop on the upper piece from back to front — pull the thread through.

3 Put the needle into the *front* of the first stitch on the right of the lower piece and through the back to the front of the next stitch on its left.

4 Repeat this with the first two stitches on the upper section and continue in this way until all the loops are joined. Close the loops taking care not to pull the row tighter than the knitted rows. Grafting takes a little practice but is quick and simple once mastered.

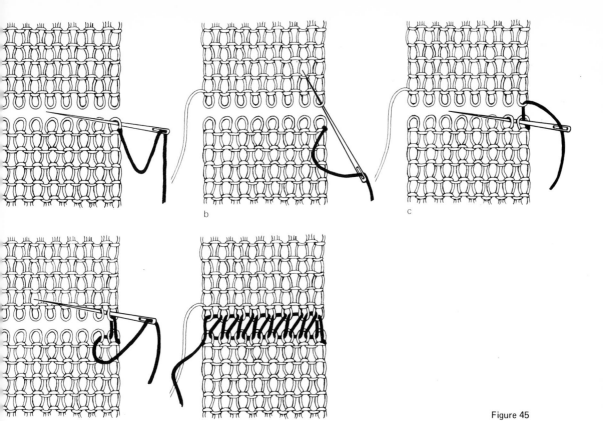

b

c

e

Figure 45

Chapter 11

KNITTING CLUBS

If you have completed one or two garments by now and have decided that machine knitting provides you with an interesting and money-saving hobby, the next step is to meet with others of similar opinions to yourself. A knitting club is not, as many would imagine, a collection of ninety year olds with shawls and baggy jumpers. Usually it is a variety of people from all walks of life and different age groups, and not all women either.

A knitting club offers you the opportunity to meet with others with similar interests to yourself. I know for a fact that if I didn't have the ladies of my knitting club to talk to, I would bore the pants off my non-knitting friends.

It is surprising how much one can learn in a couple of hours from other people's experience. Most clubs cater for everyone from the beginner to the expert, so no one is made to feel out of it.

Apart from extending your knowledge, clubs usually organize such practical money-saving ideas as 'pattern swop boxes', a pattern lending service, and accessory loan services such as skein winders, handy punches, or a 'Knit Radar'. These are all items we would like to own ourselves but cannot always afford. Clubs usually have an arrangement with a local wool supplier and are able to offer a range of coned wools at discount prices. The club organizer usually keeps in touch with new machines and accessories and often can arrange demonstrations of new models at club meetings. This gives a much better chance of seeing what a model can do than you would get in a crowded department store with husband and children in tow.

The club organizer will have a mine of information on tap, from the telephone numbers of people who wish to employ knitters to the date and place of the next wool sale, not to mention a list of people with things to sell or swop, or those wanting to buy. Many a secondhand machine has changed hands at club meetings to the mutual benefit of both parties.

Knitting clubs are non profit-making concerns, so you have no need to fear exploitation. All you will receive for the few pence of your monthly subscription is help, encouragement, and a good night out.

To find out where your nearest club meets, ask any machine stockist or manufacturer, or look in the latest machine knitting magazine.

Machines are provided at the clubs, so there will be no need to struggle on and off buses with your machine and table, and if you don't happen to own a machine, you will be equally as welcome.

Finally, if you cannot find a club in your area, you have only one choice — start one.

EVENING CLASSES

Many of the more progressive Education Authorities have realized the need to include machine knitting as an entire subject in the evening Adult Education Centres. These provide an ideal way to master the basic techniques essential to the new knitter.

Depending on the amount of interest shown, some classes progress to the more advanced techniques, the use of ribbing attachments and the mastering of pattern writing and garment design.

The prospectus for evening classes in your area can always be viewed at any library and usually you can attend for an evening to see what goes on before enrolling for a term.

Some classes are run on an instructional basis with one machine used for demonstration purposes, whilst others encourage class members to take their own machines along and knit various garments under supervision.

Evening classes are inexpensive, and the tutor is usually a dedicated knitter herself with years of experience in practical application as well as technical know-how. You will find that she will be aware of your difficulties and will be able to encourage even the most disheartened.

Chapter 12

KNITTING FOR PROFIT

Every garment completed on a knitting machine shows a profit. If you only knit for yourself and your family, the turning out of 'shop' quality garments at a fraction of today's prices makes the machine pay for itself many times over. If friends only pay for the wool and not your time you have the satisfaction of deriving pleasure from your machine without any outlay. The saving on Christmas and birthday presents alone is worthy of thought. If, like some, you wish to turn your talents to making a steady income from your machine without leaving the comfort of your own home then there are several alternatives.

Taking private orders

Once you and your family are seen wearing your machine knitted garments you will have no shortage of orders. Taking private orders is probably the most pleasant way of earning money with your machine, but care must be taken to keep the whole project on a business footing. You will come up against people who expect to pay for the wool only and not your time, and even people who don't expect to pay at all. Other disadvantages of private orders are the Aunt Alices of this world who want a royal blue polo neck sweater in double knitting with 'BAY CITY ROLLERS' splashed all over the front in purple and white. You can only find such a pattern in 4-ply and that will be a 'V' neck and the wool shop will only have French navy in the blue line that week. Take heart: all these problems can be overcome, or better still, with a little forethought they can be avoided altogether.

The secret of success is to be business-like and organized right from the outset. Set your stall out, so to speak, and start as you mean to go on.

First of all decide on your limitations. How many garments you can tackle in, say, a month, and what sort of garments. Start with easy garments such as school woollies, which are always in demand and very expensive in the shops.

Decide on your charges, not forgetting to take into account your time as well as the materials. Some people charge by the hour but this is difficult to calculate especially if you are subject to lots of interruptions.

The easiest way to price a garment is to charge by the gram. Charge so much for 4-ply, so much for 3-ply and add on a small amount for Fair Isle etc. Usually you can charge a fixed amount for sewing up, such as one price for children's garments and slightly more for an adult garment.

When someone asks you to knit for them, give them an estimate based on the cost of the materials and your time. Itemize the costs including extras such as buttons and zips. This way you will be able to knit happily knowing that you will be paid without the customer quibbling over the price. Time and money can be saved by bulk buying of wool, especially the industrially coned wool which is both excellent quality and inexpensive to buy. If you are able to buy wool in this way you can increase your profit margin by charging the usual shop prices for the wool. If possible use your own rather than wool supplied by your customers. They will turn up on your doorstep with all sorts of yarns, the most popular being last year's cricket sweater pulled out and dyed green, guaranteed to set your machine shuddering at the very sight! The standard and kindest reply to a request of this type is 'I'm sorry the machine wouldn't like it.'

Keep an order book and make extensive notes, not only of the knitting but also of your expenses and profits.

Allow yourself plenty of time to complete your orders. Tell the customer a few days longer than you think it will take you; that way she doesn't worry if you are a bit late and will be delighted if you are early.

Finally don't take on more than you can cope with. Better to have six satisfied customers than twenty irate people hounding you for unfinished garments.

To sum up: Be organized and business-like. Decide on your limitations and be firm. Keep clear records both with regard to the knitting and to your finances.

Knitting for a firm

There are many small firms producing exclusive home-knitted garments for sale in this country and for export. At first glance a job with such a firm seems ideal. You are working at home and need only do as much as you can manage, wool and patterns are provided etc. *Beware*. There are pitfalls and you need to know exactly what you are taking on. Find out:

1 What sort of garments you will be knitting. This of course will vary but you want to know whether they are mostly plain, or Fair Isle with lots of colour changes.

2 About the type of yarn that they use. It may be conveniently wound on cones ready for you to knit, on the other hand it may be in big hairy hanks waiting for you to wax and wind it. All of which takes time.

3 What sort of patterns they use. If they are radar blocks, then, if you own a radar, you can't go wrong. Check with the firm that they do their tension squares in the same way as you. If knitting patterns are used, have someone from the firm go through a pattern with you to make sure that you can follow it.

4 If the work involves any sewing up. It shouldn't do, apart from sewing in ends. This can be a bigger task than it at first seems, especially if it is a pattern with a lot of colour changes.

5 If the firm collects and delivers. It is no good spending a whole day and half of your profits trekking across town with a mountain of wool and garments.
If the firm does not collect, your knitting schedule needs to be on a monthly basis to cut down on travelling time and expenses.

6 Finally, but most important, how much do they pay and when do they pay it? The ideal is payment per garment payable on delivery. Monthly payments are suitable to most people providing that they arrive on time.

To summarize: If you can find a firm that provides good quality, ready-wound yarn, clear patterns and uncomplicated garments, and that collects and delivers and does not expect any sewing up, not to mention paying reasonable wages on time, then you are on to a good thing. You will no doubt have to compromise on one or more of these points, but if you take your time and ask around you will be able to find a firm to suit your needs.

Give yourself time to get used to the work. You will find at first that you worry about making mistakes and knit very slowly. You will soon gain confidence and speed up, and most of the employers are approachable and only too willing to give help and advice. After all it is in their interests as well as yours to have contented home knitters.

Knitting for a shop

The profit margin when knitting for a shop is quite small but if you want an outlet for your knitting it will earn you a little extra money and may lead to bigger and better things.

Your local wool shop is the obvious place, and if the owner will provide you with wool and patterns and pay you a certain amount for each garment knitted then this works well. Alternatively you can knit up your own wool and let her have the garments on a sale or return basis, in which case she takes a small percentage of the profits. The advantages of working like this are that you have a shop window in which to display your wares and you will probably get a better price for them this way than selling them from home. Another advantage is that you will most likely get repeat orders via the shop.

To recap, this way of knitting will not earn you large profits but it is a steady way of earning a few extra pennies and often it leads to other things.

Chapter 13

BEGINNERS' PATTERNS
1 Lady's Round Neck Jumper
2 Lady's Overtop
3 Lady's Tabard
4 Man's 'V' Neck Sweater
5 Child's Fair Isle Jumper
6 Child's Hat and Scarf
7 Child's Tank Top
8 Girl's Short Sleeve Jumper and Circular Skirt
9 Stockings

Where 4-ply Acrylic yarn is used the yarn is high bulk
Acrylic specially coned for knitting machines. Other 4-ply
may be used but it may take more yarn.

The wool used for the overtop was pure wool and the tabard
was knitted in 4-ply Shetland wool which must be washed
before it is measured for tension.

In the patterns the figures in brackets refer to the other sizes.
For any abbreviations see instruction book.

1 LADY'S ROUND NECK JUMPER

Sizes: 86cm 91cm 96cm (34in 36in 38in) (finished measurement)
Materials: 4-ply Acrylic. 13(14)(15) 25g balls
Tension: 28 sts 40 rows to 10cm (4in)
Tension dial: Approx 7. Rib tension 5

Pattern details optional
Cable worked over 36sts in centre as follows:

1 needle non-working	6 cable
position (NWP)	1 NWP
6 cable	6 plain
1 NWP	1 NWP
6 plain stitches	6 cable
1 NWP	1 NWP

How to knit a cable
To work a cable over 6 stitches you need 2 triple transfer
tools. Transfer the 3 stitches at the left to the transfer tool —
put the tool into your left hand and hold it up so that the
stitches slide to the bottom of the prongs. Transfer the 3
stitches at the right to the 3 needles at the left. Put the other
transfer tool back into your right hand and transfer the
stitches to the 3 right-hand needles. Bring the 6 needles out
to D (holding position) and leave the carriage setting normal
so that the needles knit back to the knitting position. Knit 10
rows.

Back

Arrange needles for 2 x 1 rib.
Cast on 126 (134 . 140) sts.
Knit 48 rows rib.
Turn up hem. Row counter 000.
Knit 120 (130 . 130) rows straight.

Shape raglan armholes
Row Counter 000.
Cast off 2 (3 . 2) sts at beginning of next 2 rows.
Decrease 1 stitch each end of alternate rows 41(43 . 46)
times.
Knit to row 86 (90 . 96).
Run work off on waste yarn.

Front

Knit as for back until row 54 (56 . 60) after beginning of
armhole shaping.

Shape neck
Put centre 20 (22 . 24) sts and all stitches at left to holding
position.
Keeping arm shaping correct decrease 1 stitch at neck edge
on every row 10 times.
Keep neck edge straight and continue with armhole shaping
until all stitches worked off.
Leave centre 20 (22 . 24) sts holding.
Shape left half to match right.
Run stitches off on waste yarn.

Sleeves (two alike)

Arrange needles for 2 x 1 rib.
Cast on 62 (64 . 66) sts.
Knit 48 rows rib.
Turn up hem. Row counter 000.
Increase 1 stitch each end of every 8th
  (6th . 6th) row 18 (21 . 22) times to 98
  (106 . 110) sts.

Knit straight to row 150 (160 . 160).
Cast off 2 (3 . 2) sts at beginning of next 2 rows.
Decrease 1 stitch each end of alternate rows
  41 (43 . 46) times.
12 (14. 14) sts remain.
Run work off on waste yarn.

Neckband

With right side of work facing pick up
  stitches round top of sleeve, front,
  sleeve, back.
Knit one row main tension.
Transfer stitches for 2 x 1 rib.

Rib tension knit 20 rows rib.
Bring all needles to knitting position.
Knit 3 rows on all needles.
Run work off on waste yarn.

To finish

Block and press with a dry cloth
  and warm iron.
Backstitch neckband.

Join raglan seams.
Join side and sleeve seams.
Give final press.

2 LADY'S OVERTOP

Size: 97 - 102cm (38 - 40in)
Materials: 17 25g balls 4-ply wool main colour 1 25g ball contrast colour
Tension: 27 sts 40 rows to 10 cm (4 in)
Tension dial: Approx 8. Rib tension 5

Pattern details

12 rows 2 colour tuck stitch
Knitmaster basic card No. 3
Any other small tuck pattern could be substituted.

Back

Cast on 128 sts.
Knit 30 rows.
Knit 1 row T. 10.
Knit 30 rows — turn up hem.

Knit straight to row 138.
Knit 12 rows pattern.
Row counter 150 — mark here for armhole.
Knit straight to row 224.

Shape shoulders
Cast off 10 sts at beginning of next 2 rows and 12 sts at
beginning of next 4 rows.
(Refer to instruction book, instead of casting shoulders off
you can hold them.)
Run centre 60 sts off on waste thread.
If shoulder stitches are holding run each shoulder off on
waste yarn.

Front

Knit as for back until row 200.
Hold centre 20 sts and all stitches to left of centre.

Shape neck
Decreaee 1 stitch at neck edge on every row 20 times.
Knit straight to row 224.
Shape shoulder as for back.
Keeping centre stitches holding, work left half to match right.
Run stitches off on waste yarn.
Join one shoulder seam.

Neckband

With right side facing, pick up stitches round front and back of neck.
Knit 1 row.
Transfer stitches for 1 x 1 rib.
Rib tension knit 20 rows rib.
Bring all needles to knitting position.
Knit 3 rows.
Run work off on waste yarn.

Sleeves (two alike)

Join second shoulder seam.
With wrong side of work facing:
Pick up stitches between marker
  threads on front and back (108 sts).
Knit one row.

Knit 12 rows pattern as for front and back.
Knit straight to row 100.
Knit 1 row T. 10.
Knit 20 rows for hem.
Cast off.

To finish
Block and press.
Sew down neckband with backstitch.

Turn up sleeve hem.
Sew side and sleeve seams.
Give final press.

3 LADY'S TABARD
Size: 91 - 97cm (36 - 38 in)
Materials: 9 25g balls 4-ply Shetland wool main colour
3 25g balls contrast colour
Tension: 29 sts 40 rows to 10cm (4 in)
ension square should be washed before measuring.
Tension dial: Approx 7

Pattern details
Any Fair Isle pattern of 30—40 rows may be used.
For the hem knit the same number of rows plus 1 row
T. 10 as for the Fair Isle pattern band.

Back
Cast on 130 sts.
Knit 35 rows.
Knit 1 row T. 10.

Start pattern. Knit 35 rows Fair Isle.
Turn up hem.
Knit straight to row 230.
Cast off.

Front Knit exactly as back.

Edges
Taking each side separately with wrong side of work facing:
Pick up stitches evenly along each side edge.
In contrast colour knit 9 rows.
Knit 1 row T. 10.
Knit 9 rows.
Pick up edge every alternate stitch to join hem.
Knit 1 row T. 10.
Cast off with latchet tool.
Knit the other 3 edges the same.

To finish
Block and press — hot iron — wet cloth.
Join shoulder seams 12cm (5 in) along.
Turn down neck edge about 1 cm.
Overlap side edges for about 5cm at waist and catch down.
Knit a circular cord about 150cm (60 in) long.
Press.

4 MAN'S 'V' NECK SWEATER

Sizes: 97cm 102cm 107cm (38in 40in 42in)
Materials: 12(13)(14) 25g balls 4-ply wool main colour
6(7)(7) 25g balls 4-ply contrast colour
Tension over stocking stitch: 28 sts 40 rows to 10 cm (4 in)
Tension dial: Approx 7. Rib tension 5
Tension dial for Fair Isle: Approx 8

Pattern details
Any Fair Isle pattern for front and back.

Back
Arrange needles for 2 x 1 rib.
Cast on 140 (148 . 154) sts.

Knit 48 rows rib.
Turn up hem. Row counter 000.
Knit 117 (126 . 126) rows straight.

Shape armholes
Row counter 000.
Cast off at beginning of next 2 rows 5 sts.
Cast off at beginning of next 2 rows 4 sts.
Cast off at beginning of next 2 rows 3 sts.
Cast off at beginning of next 2 rows 2 sts.
Decrease 1 stitch on alternate rows each end 3 (5 . 5) times.
Knit straight to row 72 (76 . 80).

Shape shoulders
At beginning of next 2 rows cast off 6 (7 . 7) sts.
At beginning of next 2 rows cast off 6 (6 . 7) sts.
At beginning of next 2 rows cast off 6 (6 . 7) sts.
At beginning of next 2 rows cast off 6 (6 . 7) sts.
At beginning of next 2 rows cast off 6 (6 . 6) sts.
Run remaining stitches off on waste yarn.

Front
Knit as back until arm shaping.
Shape armhole as for back *but at the same time*:
Hold all stitches to left of 0 in D position and shape 'V' neck as follows:
All sizes decrease 1 stitch at neck edge every 3rd row 24 times.
Knit straight at neck edge to row 72 (76 . 80).
Shape shoulder as for back.
Knit left half to match right.

Neckband
Join one shoulder seam.
Pick up with right side of work
  facing stitches along one side of
  'V' neck and back of neck.
Knit one row main tension.
Transfer stitches for 2 x 1 rib.
Rib tension knit 20 rows.

Bring all needles to B position.
Knit 3 rows on all needles.
Run work off on waste yarn.
Pick up stitches on other half of 'V' neck
  and knit neckband the same.

Sleeves (two alike)
Arrange needles for 2 x 1 rib.
Cast on 66 (68 . 70) sts.
Knit 48 rows.
Turn up hem. Row counter 000 main tension.
Increase 1 stitch each end of every 7th row 20 (20 . 21) times.
Knit straight to row 160.
At beginning of next 2 rows cast off 5 (5 . 7) sts.
Decrease 1 stitch at each end of alternate rows 22 (22 . 23) times.
Cast off 4 (3. 2) sts on alternate rows 3 (3 . 4) times.
Run off work on waste yarn.

To finish
Block and press — warm iron — dry cloth.
Join second shoulder seam.
Sew down neckband with backstitch.
Set in sleeves.
Join side and sleeve seams. Give final press.

5 CHILD'S FAIR ISLE JUMPER
Sizes: 61cm 67cm 72cm (24in 26in 28in)
Materials: 5(6)(7) 25g balls 4-ply Acrylic main colour
1 25g ball contrast colour
Tension: 28sts 40 rows to 10cm (4 in)
Tension dial: Approx 7. Rib tension 4

Pattern details
Any Fair Isle pattern about 30—40 rows long.
Start pattern immediately after rib.

Back
Arrange needles for 1 x 1 rib.
Cast on 92 (100 . 106) sts.
Knit 48 rows rib.
Turn up hem. Row counter 000.
Knit 70 (76 . 80) rows.

Shape armholes
Row counter 000.
Cast off 3 (2 . 2) sts at beginning of next 2 rows.
Decrease 1 stitch at each end of alternate rows 28 (31 . 33) times.
Knit straight until row 60 (66 . 70).
Run work off on waste yarn.

Front
Knit as for back until row 32 (40 . 44) after beginning of arm
shaping.

Shape neck
Hold centre 16 (18 . 20) sts and all sts at left of centre.
Keep raglan shaping correct.

73

Shape neck as follows:
Decrease 1 stitch at neck edge on every row 8 (8 . 8) times.
Keeping neck edge straight continue raglan shaping until all stitches worked off.
Run centre stitches off on waste yarn.

Sleeves (two alike)
Arrange needles for 1 x 1 rib.
Cast on 46 (50 . 52) sts.
Knit 48 rows rib.
Turn up hem.
Increase 1 stitch each end of every 7th (7th . 7th) row 11 (13 . 14) times.
Knit straight to row 90 (100 . 100).

Shape armholes
Row counter 000.
Cast off 3 (2 . 2) sts at beginning of next 2 rows.
Decrease 1 stitch each end of alternate rows 28 (31 . 33) times.
Knit straight to row 60 (66. 70).
Run work off on waste yarn.

Neckband
Pick up stitches round top of sleeve,
  front, sleeve, back.
Knit one row at main tension.
Transfer stitches for 1 x 1 rib.
Rib tension knit 20 rows.
Bring all needles to knitting position.
Knit 3 rows.
Run work off on waste yarn.

To Finish
Press with dry cloth and warm iron.
Join raglan seams.
Sew neckband down with backstitch.
Join side and sleeve seams.
Give final, light press.

CHILD'S HAT AND SCARF
To fit ages: 3 — 6 years.
Materials: 6 25g balls 4-ply Acrylic main colour 1 25g ball contrast colour
Tension: 48sts 10 rows to 10cm (4 in)
Tension dial: Approx 7. Rib tension 4

Pattern details
Use same Fair Isle pattern as Fair Isle jumper.

Hat
Arrange needles for 1 x 1 rib. Knit 48 rows rib.
Turn up hem. Row counter 000.
Knit 24 rows plain.
Knit 30—40 rows Fair Isle.
Knit straight to row 80.
Run work off on waste yarn.

To finish
Run a thread through top of hat and draw up top.
Remove waste yarn.
Sew side seam.
Make a pom pom and sew on top of hat.

74

Scarf

Cast on 96 sts with waste yarn.
Knit a few rows.
Join in main yarn and knit 24 rows plain.
Knit Fair Isle band.

Knit straight to row 300.
Knit Fair Isle band.
Knit 24 rows plain.
Run work off on waste yarn.

To finish

Join long seams.
Run thread through each end and
  draw ends up.

Make 2 pom poms.
Sew one on each end.
Press lightly.

7 CHILD'S TANK TOP

Sizes: 61cm 67cm 72cm (24in 26in 28in)
Materials: 4(5)(6) 25g balls 4-ply Acrylic Oddments in 2 contrast colours
Tension: 28 sts 40 rows to 10cm (4 in)
Tension dial: Approx 7. Rib tension 5

Pattern details

The single motif pattern is optional, the tank top can be
knitted plain. If the motif is used any pattern up to 60 rows
can be substituted.

Back

Arrange needles for 2 x 1 rib.
Cast on 84 (92 . 98) sts.
Knit 48 rows rib.
Turn up hem. Row counter 000.
Knit 56 (60 . 66) rows straight.
Row counter 000.

Shape armholes
Cast off 4 (4 . 5) sts at beginning of next 2 rows.
Cast off 3 (3 . 4) sts at beginning of next 2 rows.
Cast off 2 (3 . 3) sts at beginning of next 2 rows.
Cast off 1 (2 . 2) sts at beginning of next 2 rows.
Sizes 67cm and 72cm only: Cast off 1 stitch beginning of next 2 rows.
Knit straight to row 58 (62 . 66).

Shape shoulders
All sizes: Cast off 5 sts at beginning of next 6 rows.
Run remaining stitches off on waste yarn.

Front

Knit as for back to beginning of arm shaping, knitting single
motif if desired. On first row of arm shaping shape neck as follows:
Hold centre 20 sts and all stitches to left of centre.
Shape right arm as for back. *At the same time:*
Decrease 1 stitch at neck edge on every row 7 (8 . 9) times.
Continue neck edge straight until row 58 (62 . 66).
Shape shoulder as for back.
Knit left half to match right.

Neckband

Join one shoulder seam.
Right side of work facing, pick up stitches round front and back neck.
Knit one row main tension.
Transfer stitches for 2 x 1 rib.
Knit 10 rows main colour rib tension.
1 row main colour T. 10.

3 rows main colour.
3 rows contrast colour 1.
3 rows contrast colour 2.
1 row main colour.
Bring all needles to working position.
Knit 2 rows.
Run work off on waste yarn.

Armband

Join second shoulder seam.
With right side of work facing pick up stitches along armhole edge.
Knit armband as for neckband but shape ends by decreasing
1 stitch each end of alternate rows for 10 rows and then
increase 1 stitch each end of alternate rows for 10 rows.

To finish

Sew down neck and arm bands with backstitch.
Join side seams.
Press lightly.

8 GIRL'S SHORT SLEEVE JUMPER AND SKIRT

Size: To fit age 6 years
Materials: 14 25g balls 4-ply Tricel nylon
Tension: 28 sts 40 rows to 10cm (4 in)
Tension dial: Approx 8. Rib tension 6

Pattern details

A random dye is effective for this pattern.

JUMPER
Back

Arrange needles for 2 x 1 rib.
Cast on 92 sts.
Knit 48 rows rib.

Turn up hem. Row counter 000.
Knit 66 rows straight.

Shape armholes
Row counter 000.
Cast off 3 sts at beginning of next 2 rows.
Decrease 1 stitch each end of alternate rows 28 times.
Knit straight to row 60.
Run work off on waste yarn.

Front

Knit as for back until row 32 after beginning of arm shaping.

Shape neck
Hold centre 16 sts and all stitches to left of centre.
Keeping raglan arm shaping correct decrease 1 stitch at neck
edge on every row 8 times.
Keeping neck edge straight continue arm shaping until all
stitches are worked off.

Sleeves (two alike)
Arrange needles for 2 x 1 rib.
Cast on 48 sts.
Knit 30 rows rib.

Turn up hem. Row counter 000.
Increase 1 stitch each end of every
3rd row to 68 sts.
Knit 2 rows straight.

Shape raglan
Cast off 3 sts at beginning of next 2 rows.
Decrease 1 stitch at each end of alternate rows 28 times.
Knit straight to row 60.
Run work off on waste yarn.

Neckband
Pick up stitches round top of sleeve — front — sleeve — back.
Knit one row at main tension.
Transfer stitches for 2 x 1 rib.
Knit 20 rows rib.
Bring all needles to working position.
Knit 3 rows.
Run work off on waste yarn.

To finish
Block and press.
Join raglan seams.
Sew down neckband with backstitch.
Join side and sleeve seams.
Give final press.

CIRCULAR SKIRT
Size: Waist 67cm (26 in) length 33cm (13 in)

With waste yarn cast on 116 sts.
Knit a few rows — carriage at right.
With main yarn knit 10 rows.
**Bring 10 needles at left to D (holding position).
Set carriage — front levers on I to hold.
Knit one row to left.
Always taking yarn round inside needles in D position knit
to the right.
*Repeat these 2 rows 9 times altogether.
Knit 20 rows on all needles.
**Repeat from ** to ** 13 times more.
And then from ** to * once more.
Knit 10 rows straight.
Run work off on waste yarn.

Graft skirt seam either by hand or by machine as per instruction book.
Turn down 2cm and insert elastic for waistband.
Turn up hem as required.
Press.

9 STOCKINGS

Size: To fit shoe size 5
Materials: 9 25g balls 4-ply Acrylic (2 balls red, 2 balls white, 5 balls blue)
Tension dial: Approx 6. Rib tension 5

Arrange needles for 2 x 1 rib.
Cast on 106 sts in main colour.
Knit 40 rows rib. Row counter 000.
(Work the colour changes every 10 rows 12 times and then every 5 rows up to row 200. Work in 3 colours.)
Decrease 1 stitch each end of next and every following 10th row 12 times.
Decrease 1 stitch each end of every following 5th row 7 times (68sts).
Knit straight to row 220 finished stripes at row 200 and continuing in main colour.
Decrease 1 stitch FF at each end of next and every 5th row 5 times altogether (58 sts).
Increase 1 stitch each end of alternate rows 5 times (68 sts).
Knit 3 rows.

Shape toe and heel

Counting from left push 51 needles to D (holding position).
With waste yarn knit a few rows over 17 sts at right and release from the machine.
Put 17 needles at left to C position and run off on waste yarn.
Work foot on remaining 34 needles.
Knit straight 50 rows.
Carriage at right and always taking yarn round inside needle in D position put 1 needle opposite the carriage end to D position on the next 16 rows.
Always taking yarn round inside needle in D position put 1 needle opposite carriage end back to C position on next 16 rows.
Knit 50 rows straight.
Shape heel as for toe by repeating from * to*.
Knit 2 rows.
Run work off on waste yarn.
Graft heel.
Sew up and press lightly.

Chapter 14

MISCELLANEOUS HANDY HINTS

During the time that it has taken to compile this book I have been picking the brains of other knitters and several handy hints have come to light. The best way for me to thank the people who have helped me is to pass on the favourite hints to you.

Never trust to memory:

Even the most experienced knitter will tell you to commit to paper anything that you want to remember. Write it in a way that you will be able to understand in the future. Avoid too many abbreviations, you might forget what they stand for!

Care of your machine

An easy way to oil the edges of the cams is to apply the oil with a nail varnish brush or some other small, soft-bristled brush.

Knitting with difficult yarns

Before casting on by hand with a particularly fine or difficult yarn, e.g. fine bouclé wool or rayon, make an open edge cast on with waste yarn and knit a few rows. Break off the waste yarn and rethread with the main yarn. Bring the needles out to D position and make your hand cast on.

Another difficulty with fine, silky yarns, knitted for a cone, is that the yarn tends to drop off the cone and fall in heaps around the base. There are two ways of tackling this particular knitters' nightmare:

If the yarn is smooth and silky, pull a piece of old nylon stocking (or tights) over the cone and this will hold the yarn on the cone without interfering with the flow.

If the yarn is hard and bobbly, e.g. viscose yarn, then, strange as it may seem, a piece of fur fabric wrapped round the base of the cone will stop the yarn from dropping off the cone. I have no idea how this works but I can assure you from experience that it does.

Punch lace

It is useful to know that a garment knitted in a lacy stitch takes less wool than the same garment knitted in stocking stitch.

Holding stitches

Sometimes when you are holding stitches, particularly when shaping a neckline, the action of the brushes passing continually over the held stitches causes a furry line where

79

the wool has been 'fluffed up'. On a light coloured garment it can also cause an oil mark. To avoid this, stick a piece of Sellotape along the work close to the sinkers where the stitches are held. Put Sellotape on both sides of the knitting and it will keep the piece free of oil and fluff.

Blocking and pressing
Use a set square and draw a straight line in biro on your pressing cloth and another line at right angles to the first one. You can then pin out the bottom and one side of a garment and be sure that you are pinning it straight. Alternatively use a ruler and pin the work using the ruler to keep the edges straight.

Sewing up on a machine
If the knitted fabric tends to catch in the foot of the machine sew on a piece of fine tissue paper. This can be easily removed once the seam is complete.

Single motif knitting
If you are knitting a single motif on a garment and it is quite a distance from the edge of the motif to the end of the row, you may find you get some tangling of the second yarn around the brushes. To avoid this, stop the carriage once you are past the motif, remove the second yarn from feeder two and just pull it a little towards you, carry on across the row and back again and rethread feeder two with the second yarn just before you knit across the motif.

List of suppliers

Bedford Sewing and Knitting Machines Ltd,
13 Lime Street, Bedford, Bedfordshire

The Direct Wool Group,
P.O. Box No 46,
Bradford, West Yorkshire

Mailyarns Ltd,
38 High Street,
Syston,
Leicester, Leicestershire

Weaverknits Ltd,
276-278 Main Road,
Sutton-at-Hone,
Dartford, Kent

Argyll Wools Ltd,
Priestley Mills,
Pudsey, West Yorkshire

Hayfield Yarns,
Hayfield Textiles Ltd,
Hayfield Mills,
Glusburn,
Nr Keighley, Yorkshire